The Christian's Journey Through ___ soul written by a practicing physician and highly trained minister. It beautifully depicts in an inspiring and instructive way the author's encounter with loss, engagement with grief, and celebration of hope. A doctor of ministry and a doctor of medicine, Dr. Carol Peters-Tanksley informs, instructs, and pastors her readers with a sound, biblical understanding of death and dying and deep insights into the workings of human body, mind, and spirit. *The Christian's Journey Through Grief* is a must-read for individuals facing loss and grief, and those who wish to minister to them.

—THOMSON K. MATHEW, DMIN, EDD
PROFESSOR EMERITUS AND FORMER DEAN
ORAL ROBERTS UNIVERSITY GRADUATE SCHOOL OF
THEOLOGY AND MINISTRY

Sooner or later we will all find ourselves facing a season of grief. Dr. Carol's book *The Christian's Journey Through Grief* is written for the person who is in the wake of despair that often follows loss. This book will help lead readers out of what Dr. Carol calls "the dark valley of grief" and into the healing and growth that comes through God. Our hope is in Jesus, and Dr. Carol uses His teachings to help us find strength in troubled times.

—JOE CHAMPION
SENIOR PASTOR, CELEBRATION CHURCH

Dr. Carol's personal journey through grief, her unique combination of gifts as a medical doctor and a doctor of ministry, and her transparency make her an authoritative voice on the topic of grief. Anyone who is going through grief, has gone through grief, or wants to help others through the grieving process will benefit greatly from this book. Caregivers, chaplains, pastors, connect group leaders, and grief coaches as well as the bereaved will find this work insightful. She explores the gamut of the grieving process from the "work of grief" to the biology of grief, and she does so from a biblical worldview. She shares her personal coping mechanisms and is sure to remind the reader that Christians are not exempt from grief but own a hope that is unique to those who know Christ. Share this book with those you love.

—BRENDA C. CHAND, DMIN
FOUNDER, DREAM RELEASER COACHING

I found *The Christian's Journey Through Grief* to be profoundly practical and informative. It traces the natural course of grieving following the death of a loved one. It is true to the biblical record of God's care for the children of God. It provides specific actions people can take to move through the painful process of grieving. It is well-written, and it provides hope!

All of this is consistent with what I know to be true about Dr. Carol. Her compassion has been evident to me for years. Her scholarly approach to medicine and to seeking understanding of the emotional difficulties Christians face has led her to plumb the depths of both, just as Chancellor Oral Roberts suggested: one hand for prayer, another for medicine and science.

Perhaps most importantly she has added to her academic,

scientific, and ministry background her own experiences of grief and confusion. She has made herself vulnerable to those who read this book. What an unbeatable combination—medicine, biblical training, and personal experience. I applaud her for writing this book.

—EDWARD E. DECKER JR., PHD
TENURED PROFESSOR OF CHRISTIAN COUNSELING—RETIRED
ORAL ROBERTS UNIVERSITY GRADUATE SCHOOL OF
THEOLOGY AND MINISTRY

Speaking from both personal and professional experience, Dr. Carol presents a practical and compassionate discussion of the journey through grief that offers understanding, help, and hope. I highly recommend her work for anyone who is trying to recover from an experience of loss.

—BILL BUKER, DMIN, PHD, LPC
ASSOCIATE DEAN, ORAL ROBERTS UNIVERSITY
GRADUATE SCHOOL OF THEOLOGY AND MINISTRY

Grief cannot be denied. It should not be denied. To acknowledge that it exists is crucial. It is even more crucial that it be dealt with in the proper way. As a pastor for many years and now the leader of a ministry whose members are often thrust into the darkness of grief, I have seen some react with actions as diverse as selling the house, becoming a recluse, and marrying immediately. There is a proper way to deal with this monster, and no one can address this better than Dr. Carol. She has lived it in every way. And she has addressed it in the proper way. Join Dr. Carol as she leads you to victory over this most insidious foe. She does not do so alone but with a gentle spirit while being led by the most high God. Enjoy your journey to wholeness with someone who knows what she is talking about.

—REV. DR. HOWARD S. RUSSELL
PRESIDENT AND CEO, CHRISTIAN HEALTHCARE MINISTRIES

Just as Jesus walked the road to Emmaus with the disciples, in *The Christian's Journey Through Grief* Dr. Carol will walk with you through your journey to process your grief. Using Dr. Carol's transparent teaching about her own walk of grief, the Holy Spirit will minister to you, giving you revelation and comfort. As I reviewed this manuscript, the Lord fulfilled the principles of Luke 24 even in my own life. I invite you to open your heart to the Lord as you walk with Dr. Carol and the Holy Spirit on your individual journey through grief.

Thank you, Dr. Carol, for being an instrument of the Lord, as we all deal with journeys through grief.

—DONALD R. TREDWAY, MD, PHD
FORMER CHAIRMAN OF THE DEPARTMENT OF OBSTETRICS
AND GYNECOLOGY
ORAL ROBERTS UNIVERSITY SCHOOL OF MEDICINE
FOUNDER OF RESURRECTION MINISTRIES INC.

THE CHRISTIAN'S
JOURNEY
Through
GRIEF

THE CHRISTIAN'S

JOURNEY

—— *Through* ——

GRIEF

CAROL PETERS-TANKSLEY, MD, DMin

CHARISMA
HOUSE

Most CHARISMA HOUSE BOOK GROUP products are available at special quantity discounts for bulk purchase for sales promotions, premiums, fund-raising, and educational needs. For details, write Charisma House Book Group, 600 Rinehart Road, Lake Mary, Florida 32746, or telephone (407) 333-0600.

THE CHRISTIAN'S JOURNEY THROUGH GRIEF
by Carol Peters-Tanksley, MD, DMin
Published by Charisma House
Charisma Media/Charisma House Book Group
600 Rinehart Road
Lake Mary, Florida 32746
www.charismahouse.com

Library of Congress Cataloging-in-Publication Data:
An application to register this book for cataloging has been submitted to the Library of Congress.
International Standard Book Number: 978-1-62999-599-1
E-book ISBN: 978-1-62999-600-4

19 20 21 22 23 — 987654321
Printed in the United States of America

To my husband, Al Tanksley,

For loving and cherishing me with your whole heart,

For investing all of yourself in me,

I love you and miss you.

You are and always will be the wind beneath my wings.

CONTENTS

INTRODUCTION

DEATH, YOU MAY *think you have won. Yes, the wounds you have inflicted are deep. And we will mourn as we nurse those wounds. But in truth you have lost again! While to human eyes you may seem to have won this battle, in reality you have already lost the war. And every life you take—temporarily—is but another nail in your own coffin. Death, you will be destroyed! And Al Tanksley, along with me and all the rest of us who trust in Jesus, will live forever. Then where, O death, will be your sting? Where, O grave, will be your victory?"*

With those words I declared once more the death of death. Facing family and friends, my husband's casket draped in the stars and stripes behind me, I thanked Al for having loved me so completely. Then I dug deep to find the faith and hope to speak the words you just read through pain that was beyond description. I knew the days and months ahead would be hard, and they were. Very hard.

As I write these words, it is Easter. This morning I visited the cemetery where I laid my husband's body to rest, and through my tears I sang resurrection hymns over his grave. I looked around at all the other graves and thought yet again that too many people are being buried. A woman visiting her mother's grave came over and spoke to me. She was struggling to imagine anything beyond the pain of her loss, anything beyond that day. I pointed to the words engraved on the back of my husband's headstone.[1]

> Death is swallowed up in victory.
> O death, where is thy sting?
> O grave, where is thy victory?
> 1 Corinthians 15:54–55

I told her, "I don't know how anyone can go on who does not know Jesus. It's only because He is alive that we can look forward to the resurrection. Only because He lives do we have hope." I pray my words somehow encouraged and comforted her.

As I sat there looking at all the graves, the reality of the resurrection hit me all over again. Real people are buried here, but there is a tomb that is empty. After Jesus' death and resurrection, the angel told His disciples, "Why do you seek the living among the dead? He is not here, but has risen!" (Luke 24:5–6, MEV). At the cross Jesus declared the end of sin, and in the resurrection He declared the end of death. Not yet, of course, but their end will come.

Because of Easter, cemeteries are temporary.

Yet to our human senses death seems so final. So heavy. So impenetrable. So dark. Some speak of finding closure after the death of a loved one. Those of us grieving may want to scream, "Closure? What's that?" Most people shrink from death. We do everything possible to avoid thinking about it, talking about it, seeing it, or accepting it. Yet the Bible says the fear of death is bondage (Heb. 2:15).

When the funeral is done—the ashes spread or the body lowered into the ground—it all feels so final. It's over—ashes to ashes, dust to dust. But is it really over? Our final is God's temporary. In the full scheme of things cemeteries are temporary. There will be no graves to visit in heaven or in the new earth. There will be no funerals, no headstones, no urns, no ashes, no mausoleums, no undertakers, no caskets, no hearses, no hymns meant to comfort those left behind.

In only a little while our tears will be wiped away.

For those who believe in Jesus, death is temporary.

If you're grieving right now, you may wish *temporary* meant your anguish would quickly go away and things could go back to the way they were. But your loved one is gone, and death doesn't feel temporary at all. Right now the only thing you may be aware of is your heart crying, "Just make the pain stop!"

Your head may know that Jesus has already dealt with death, yet your heart feels a grief that's too big to express. The people who gathered around you when your loved one first died are going on with their lives now, but you still find it difficult to even think. Your emotions are all tangled: regrets, anger, loneliness, confusion, sadness, fear, anxiety, exhaustion, hopelessness, relief—it's too much. It may feel as though your faith is on life support. Like Mary and Martha, you may be crying, "Lord, if You had been here, my [loved one] would not have died" (John 11:21, 32, MEV).

How can you make it through this dark valley of grief? What are you supposed to do now? Is it really supposed to hurt this much if you're a believer? You can't imagine getting through the next hour, let alone the next year. You grasp at anything that promises to make the pain go away even for a moment.

The witness of the New Testament and of those who have believed in Jesus during the past two thousand-plus years is that believers still grieve. Death still hurts—a lot! But we do "not grieve as others who have no hope" (1 Thess. 4:13, MEV). We grieve, but we grieve differently.

This book is about that difference.

It's about going through the dark valley and finding your way to the other side.

It's about learning to embrace excruciating pain and irrepressible hope at the same time.

It's about riding the waves of grief that threaten to drown you and feeling God's hand rescue you.

It's about doing the human work of grief while giving God full opportunity to bring real healing.

It's about embracing the "not OK-ness" of death and eventually choosing to go on living anyway.

It's about grieving but grieving differently because Jesus is alive and with you.

In the chapters ahead you will, from time to time, notice the same idea discussed more than once in different contexts. That's because your brain may not well remember something from, say, chapter 2 by the time you get to, say, chapter 5. When an idea fits more than one part of the grief journey, I mention it again.

Your grief journey will be your own. No one else can walk it for you. It will be confusing and irregular at times. There are unique elements of your past with your loved one, the way your loved one died, and your present circumstances that color your grief in a way only you can fully appreciate.

But you do not have to make your way alone. Others have walked this journey before you—I am one of them. Let me put my hand on your shoulder. Let this book be a lifeline when nothing much makes sense. Let me hold the Christ-light for you, walking one step ahead of you as you make your way through this darkness, confident that you can find the light again—the light that never stopped shining.

CHAPTER 1
GRIEF AS A JOURNEY

Only people who are capable of loving
strongly can also suffer great sorrow.
—LEO TOLSTOY

THEY SAY YOU'RE never supposed to start a book or story
or chapter with "The phone rang," but the phone did
ring, waking me from an exhausted sleep at 2:00 a.m. My
husband's son had stayed with him at the hospital to allow
me a few hours at home. Now I heard his voice say, "You
need to come to the hospital."

And three hours later I returned home a widow.

Nothing can fully prepare you for the experience of grief.
Even if your loved one's death was not a complete surprise,
your world has shockingly changed forever. Your life, your
thoughts, your time, your belongings, your emotions, your
daily routine, your faith—suddenly they all feel foreign. It
can be difficult to even recognize yourself. What do you
do now?

The reality of grief you find yourself in is almost never
what you thought it would be like. Your world has been

1

ruptured in a way you never could have anticipated. A part of you is gone. Maybe it feels like *all* of you is gone! You might wish you could wake up from this nightmare and discover it was just a dream. But that isn't possible.

"Grief is a journey." I heard and read that statement many times in the early days after my husband's death, and I hated the idea. I didn't want to go on a journey! I wanted someone to tell me what to do. I wanted to know how to get through this quickly, how to stop hurting, how to do grief "right" so I wouldn't keep struggling. With billions of people having lost loved ones in this world, surely someone somewhere had figured it out and could tell me what I needed to know.

But no one could tell me, and no one can tell you either. No one had your relationship with your loved one. No one felt quite the same love, dysfunction, joy, quirkiness, humor, tension, security, pain, or longing that characterized your relationship with your spouse, child, parent, sibling, or best friend. Yes, others have experienced all those emotions. But no one has experienced them the way you have. Your relationship was unique, and your grief will be unique as well.

That may not feel very comforting right now, but hopefully it at least affirms that others have felt the aloneness you're feeling as you grieve. The very best that friends, family, and fellow believers can do in supporting you does not take that feeling away. It's your loss. Others can do much, and we'll talk about how to access the support the body of Christ is designed to offer a little later, but others cannot take your loss away from you.

Grief may feel like you're walking through a dark valley without a map, and then suddenly any flicker of light goes away. You don't recognize where you are, you're not sure there's a "there" to walk toward, and you can't see one step in front of you. When you do try to move, you keep banging into crags and crevices, hitting your head on branches, and falling over unseen rocks. Or it may seem this valley is flooded and you're about to drown. Either way, it's tempting to just quit, to give up and die, unsure there's any way out.

But don't quit. You may well need to slow down. You may make a few wrong turns and have to retrace some steps occasionally. You will hit some dead ends. Some boulders will seem too big to get past. Some passages will seem too narrow to navigate through. Sometimes you will have to pause and nurse your wounds a bit before continuing. Sometimes the air will suddenly change and take your breath away. But don't quit.

As dark as it is for you, as paralyzed and alone as you feel, as impossible as it seems to take one more step, that's exactly what you need to do. The only way to make it through this valley is by taking one small step at a time. This book will be one tool to help you do that. It will help you understand how your grief is not nearly as unique as it seems. It will show you what taking one more step looks like and offer you support as you do so. It will help you know where to direct your precious and limited energy in a way that will help you move forward along this journey.

The Role of Time

It's been said that time heals all wounds. That's not true. Some people give up, stop living, and remain stuck in the dark valley of grief. Some wounds become infected, begin to stink, and spread their darkness and pain to everything and everyone around them. Not everyone comes out of this place of pain.

But that doesn't have to be you. It's your choice. The wounds of your grief do not have to stink. You don't have to be the one stuck in your pain. Healing is available, but it's not automatic. You do not find healing simply because time passes but as a result of what you do with that time. Doing the work of grief will allow healing to come. Personally, I didn't like that idea one bit! But I learned that doing the work of grief does lead you out of the dark valley.

Your energy is limited, and there may be other aspects of life that demand your attention right now also. But remember that the way out is through. Doing the work of grief means intentionally addressing the things this book talks about such as reviewing your loss, embracing your emotions, learning to care for yourself, and discovering how to take God on the journey with you. You don't have to take up residence in the dark valley. You will not be able to ignore it; indeed, you shouldn't. But keep going.

> **You do not find healing simply because time passes but as a result of what you do with that time.**

The journey through grief probably seems long and impossible right now. Know that in this journey it matters very little how quickly you move forward; it only matters that you keep moving, however hesitatingly and slowly. This book will help you know how to do that and give you some tools to keep on doing that.

I encourage you to decide right now that you will keep walking. Some days that will be one tiny baby step forward. Some days it will feel as though you've slipped backward. Some days you may feel as though you've moved further along this journey than you realized. The important thing is that you keep placing one foot in front of the other. If you do that, I guarantee you will not remain in this dark valley forever.

God Is With You on the Journey

The morning I arrived home from the hospital a widow, I sat down with a cup of coffee and my Bible. I opened it to 1 Corinthians 15, Paul's treatise on death and resurrection. I felt lost. My head had known that barring an unusual miracle, this day would come, and I did not doubt God would be there for me. But my heart desperately needed a touch point, something to hold on to. That day and in the weeks and months that followed, I desperately wished for God to take away the pain. I wanted God to magically bring me out of the valley of grief and make me all OK again.

He didn't. And He probably won't for you either. Death hurts. It's supposed to hurt. And we'll talk more about that in the next chapter.

But I discovered something that is more powerful than the relief of pain. I discovered that hope and pain can coexist. That's one of the biggest differences about grief for the believer. The sting of death hurts just as bad. The loss is as great. Your heart is as raw and bleeding as anyone else's. You are as confused, overwhelmed, and exhausted as anyone could be. You feel like part of you, half of you, all of you is ripped away.

Yet at the same time, sometimes in the very same instant, you have hope—a hope rising from somewhere deep in your soul that even death cannot take away or even tarnish. It's a hope that says, "I know that I know that I know this is not the end," even when everything around you looks and feels like it's the end. It's a hope that believes everything your senses are telling you in the darkest moments is not the whole story.

Too many people, I think, imagine that faith in Jesus should prevent or quickly remove the pain of grief. They think if you truly are a believer, your grief will not be a difficult journey and your wounds will magically just not hurt very much. That's simply not true. The hope and faith we have as believers does not lessen the pain. We hurt just as much! Sometimes I think we may even hurt more; God's love has softened our hearts to the point that we care and love more, so the pain of death is especially excruciating.

But faith provides us something to go along with the pain. The hope we have is not diminished by the pain of grief. I'm not sure anyone who is not walking through the dark valley of grief can fully appreciate how it's possible to experience both overwhelming pain and irrepressible hope at the same time. Ambushes of grief and ambushes of hope can sometimes chase each other like waves crashing on the shore of your soul. Hope does not lessen the pain, and pain cannot dim the hope.

An acquaintance of mine experienced the death of her husband about three years before Al passed away. When she learned of my grief, she wrote me a surprisingly short note: "Nobody but Jesus can help you now." To some that may sound callous, but it was perhaps the kindest and most understanding thing she could have said. Yes, it's absolutely vital that you reach out and accept support from others on your journey through this dark valley, and we'll talk about that later in this book. But pain is perhaps the loneliest thing in the world. No other human being can fully "go there" with you.

But Jesus can. He's the only One who truly can. And He wants to.

Your faith may be shaken with the death of your loved one, and allowing Jesus to "go there" with you may seem impossible right now. You may have some deep questions to wrestle over with God as you move along this journey. You may feel angry at Him. None of that is a surprise to Him or makes Him love you any less. His shoulders are big enough to carry you regardless of how long or convoluted your grief journey is or may become. He's still inviting you to "go there" and to allow Him to go there with you.

When God Seems Silent

"God with us" is a powerful concept. The angel who talked with Joseph about the coming birth of Jesus said, "They shall call His name Immanuel," which means, "God with us" (Matt. 1:23, MEV). That's who He is. It's why He came—to be with you even in your grief.

Taking God with you on this journey may not immediately seem comforting. What if you're in a place where any hope you had seems completely obscured by your grief? What if your faith is hanging on by a thread, if it's even there at all? What if your relationship with God has never been all that close, and now you don't sense any solid ground beneath you holding you up? I hope this book will be a helpful guide through the valley of grief, whatever your previous experience as a believer may have been. For the remainder of this chapter let's look at some of the things that could be keeping you from feeling or seeing Him, and how can you take God with you on this journey, whether or not you've gone through anything with Him in the past.

Your beliefs about God and grief

What you believe about God will certainly impact your experience of grief. Your head knowledge about God isn't nearly as impactful on this journey as what your heart deeply believes about Him. The experience of grief may expose some of your beliefs about God that you had not previously realized were there. Do you suspect He's not really all that interested in what you're going through? Do you see Him as a heavenly "bad guy" who is using your loved one's death to punish you? Do you think that if He truly cared about the overwhelming pain you're experiencing, He would do something to take it away quickly? Perhaps you think He's not as strong as many people seem to think and is essentially powerless to do anything about pain and evil, especially your pain.

I imagine that must have been how Mary and Martha felt when they met Jesus four days after their brother, Lazarus, died. They cried out, "Lord, if You had been here, my brother would not have died" (John 11:21, 32, MEV). Or to put it in a language many of us use today, "Why?"

We'll talk more about dealing with anger at God in a later chapter. For now let me encourage you to make the choice to take God with you on this journey anyway. Don't ignore or discount your questions; they're a reasonable response to your experience of grief. But realize also that as you keep walking through this dark valley, your heart and mind *will* change. You will come to understand new things and experience new feelings. Make the decision to keep your troubled thoughts as questions instead of making them final statements. In addition to other things you will learn on this journey, you may discover some new things about God as well. Remain open to that.

If your belief is strong that God is good all the time, you have a touch point already that will help you during this journey. But your mind, body, emotions, and life are still traumatized. God understands that. This journey will change your faith; it's possible for that change to make your faith stronger. Don't neglect to do the work of grief.

When you begin from a place of trust in God, He can use this journey through grief in ways you cannot yet imagine. He weeps with you. He will not leave you alone.

Intellectual instead of heart-level faith

Perhaps your previous life as a Christian has been a cerebral experience, pretty much characterized by statements of truth and trying to live a "good" lifestyle. The overwhelming emotions associated with grief may seem to be in a completely different category than your faith has ever had to address before. How can a faith that lived in your head help you now when you feel as though you can't breathe and your heart has been ripped apart?

Throughout Scripture we see God's friends bringing their deepest emotions to Him. Jesus experienced all the strong feelings you and I do. He does not want your relationship with Him to be only an intellectual and behavioral one; He wants to connect with you in the feeling and emotional areas of life also. He's all about the heart, after all. And what could touch the heart at a deeper level than grief?

If you've never allowed your emotions to flow out in God's presence, this is the time to learn to do that. In church, or even better, while alone in your bedroom or outside in nature, just start talking to Him. Let yourself weep in His presence. God treasures the tears of His children. If you need to yell or scream, do that. Don't put a filter on your words or feelings. Be you—the grieving, confused, tired, hurting you—in His presence.

After a period of weeping, yelling, or whatever else, you

may feel empty, exhausted, spent. When you do, just stay there. Don't rush out of God's presence; stay there in the quiet. Sometimes you may not feel anything. Other times you may sense God gently saying, "I'm here." Occasionally you may hear Him speak something more specific or direct to your heart. Give Him that chance. Stay there long enough for your soul to get quiet, and allow Jesus' sweet presence through His Spirit to minister to you.

Not every time you pray will you leave with a clear sense of emotional comfort. But when you keep returning to His presence over and over, God will speak to you.

God hasn't been a big part of your life.

Taking God with you on this journey through grief may seem like a foreign idea. Perhaps you've only thought about faith occasionally, and you're a Christian because, well, it's been easier to think of yourself that way because of your family, work environment, or whatever. You know a little about what a Christian is supposed to do or believe, but having a relationship with God has never been an especially big part of your life.

This experience of grief opens parts of your soul you probably didn't know existed. You may feel desperate for *something*, and you wonder if maybe God has some answers you hadn't seriously considered before.

Let me be one to affirm that God does have the answers, even for your grief. My saying so may not mean very much to you right now, and that's OK. But if my faith and that of others who have taken God along as we walk this grief journey can give you even a tiny measure of hope, then borrow a little of our faith for right now. Those of us who have chosen to take God with us have found that He doesn't remove the pain, not yet anyway. But He makes a difference, and I want that difference for you.

Let me suggest you give God a chance. That's perhaps why you picked up this book. Your hurting heart can provide an opportunity to connect with God in a very special way.

How to Walk Forward

Think of this as a guidebook. It won't provide all the answers to your *why* questions, but it will provide some framework for you to wrestle with those questions as you do your grief work. Intentionally devoting time and energy to working through the thoughts, emotions, memories, and challenges grief brings is hard; that's why it's called grief work. This book will point out some things you may experience as you journey through the valley of grief, and there will be some suggestions on how to do the work of grief along the way. You'll also be invited to think about how this journey may impact your faith and relationship with God.

Here are a few brief and important suggestions to keep in mind as you move forward.

- Take your time. Remember, there are no medals for speed in getting through the valley of grief. Don't worry about how long it's taking you. Just keep taking one small step at a time.

- Decide to do the work of grief. Remember, your healing will depend on what you choose to do during the time that passes. Take a few minutes each day, or perhaps a few hours each week, to focus on doing specific grief work. We'll talk about what that might look like in a later chapter.

- If the Bible means anything to you at all, make reading it part of your daily routine. Your mind may not be able to grasp much of what you read right now. It may seem empty. But put a few scriptures from God's Word in your mind every day. If nothing else, open to Psalms and read just a couple verses.

- Talk to God about your journey. God is patient, and there's no "right" or "wrong" way to pray at this time. But I encourage you to talk to God every day, even if it's only for a moment. If nothing else just tell Him how you feel today and ask Him to keep walking with you on this journey.

Yes, grief is an unwelcome intruder that has launched you on a journey through a dark and confusing valley. This isn't something you ever would have chosen, but you are not the first person to walk this path, and you will not be the last. Let me and others who have gone through this journey offer some touch points, some reassurance, and most of all, some hope.

The dark valley will not last forever. Just keep walking.

TWO STEPS FORWARD

At the end of each chapter you'll find a couple suggestions for how to apply the material to your grief journey. Your mind is likely struggling to think clearly, and these simple steps may help you find focus and hope.

1. Get a journal that you can use during your journey. Spend a few minutes writing about what your loved one meant to you.

2. In your journal write a few sentences as a prayer to God. Let Him know how you are feeling right now—angry, sad, lonely, confused, or whatever.

CHAPTER 2
IT HURTS. A LOT!

No one ever told me that grief felt so like fear.
—C. S. Lewis, *A Grief Observed*

GOD CREATED YOU and me as unique, integrated, whole human beings. What affects one part of you affects every other part. You can't separate the physical, mental, emotional, and spiritual parts of yourself any more than you can separate the flour, sugar, oil, and salt from a loaf of bread.

And that is never truer than when you are walking the journey through grief.

Many people wonder if their grief response is normal. If by "normal" you mean your body won't do what it's supposed to, your thoughts don't know where to land, your emotions are difficult or impossible to predict or control, you feel overwhelmed by things that normally would not have bothered you, and your connection with God seems all messed up, then the answer is yes. Messed up, confused, and totally out of sorts is normal.

Remember, we were created for eternity, not for grief.

This experience is not what God built you for originally. Everything about death and loss goes against the way life was supposed to be. God has gifted you with what you need to go through this journey, but it's completely normal when your body, mind, and soul don't know what to do next. You're not supposed to know. There's no hard-wiring in your system that says, "This is what to do when grief comes." That's why it feels like a dark valley.

In this world we may be tempted to think of death as "normal" because that's what happens to every living thing, including people. But in God's universe as a whole, death is not normal. So don't let the strangeness of how death and grief feel persuade you that there's something wrong with you. You're not weird; you're grieving.

You will respond to the loss of your loved one in a unique way. But you will almost certainly "feel" the grief in your body, mind, relationships, and spiritual life. Looking at some of the ways people going through grief have responded in these various areas may help you be aware of and embrace your own responses to grief.

Physical Responses to Grief

Your body will get some fallout as a result of your loved one's death. On the scale of stress the death of someone close to you ranks at the very top. Extremely high levels of stress hormones coursing through your blood vessels and entering every cell of your body, overwhelming thoughts and feelings that get passed to your whole body through your nervous system, the enormous "newness" of existence without your loved one—it's more than your body can absorb without some major responses. Those responses often include the following.

Sleep disruption

One of the most common body functions to become altered during grief is sleep. There are some physiological reasons for that. One of the purposes of stress hormones is to keep you alert, and you can't make those hormones go away simply by wanting them to. As a result you may feel exhausted but not be able to fall asleep, or you may wake up and not be able to go back to sleep. The stress hormones are doing their job.

Your mind is also working overtime trying to process everything. When you try to shut down long enough to sleep, the decreased stimulation often allows your mind to go into overdrive. You may find yourself ruminating over things that happened or didn't happen with your loved one, riding waves of different emotions as they wash over you, or feeling anxious about all the things you will have to do, figure out, and manage now that your loved one is gone.

As some of the initial stress subsides enough for you to sleep, you may find yourself sleeping more than you ever did previously. If your loved one died after a long illness, you may be physically and mentally exhausted from care-taking responsibilities, which adds to your need for sleep. Your body also needs sleep to repair itself from the effects of the stress hormones associated with grief. And one of the expressions of depression can also be sleeping more than normal.

How long you spend in the "unable to sleep" phase may vary from days to months, and your subsequent need for increased sleep will also vary. It took about nine months for my sleep pattern to return to something near normal; that's a shorter time than many people experience and longer than others. Give yourself some grace here. We'll talk more about rest in the coming chapter.

Other physical symptoms

If you have any medical conditions, your symptoms may increase while your grief is relatively fresh. If you have diabetes, for example, your blood sugar may fluctuate more than normal. Heart disease or breathing symptoms may worsen if you have cardiovascular or respiratory problems. Arthritis, chronic pain, or any other illness may temporarily worsen. The rate of hospitalization goes up for those grieving a loved one's death. Grief affects your immune system, and you may be more susceptible to such "simple" illnesses as a cold or the flu.

Physical pain is a common response to any major stress, including grief. Headaches, back pain, stomach pain, etc. may begin or become worse than before. Your GI system can be especially sensitive to the stress of grief. You may have absolutely no appetite or find yourself eating more junk food than you usually do. You may feel symptoms of nausea, diarrhea, or constipation. Your energy level may be in the basement, and you may find it difficult to accomplish even the simplest tasks.

Many of these physical symptoms may slowly subside as the initial stress of grief begins to lessen. The decrease in these physical symptoms may be uneven; you may feel better for a little while, and then all your symptoms may worsen again. Such a roller coaster in your physical responses to grief is very common. In the middle of your grief it may feel as though your body is betraying you. Be gentle with yourself. Slow down! Your body may well be experiencing a level of stress as great as after a major surgery or traumatic accident. You will need to take extra care of yourself during this time, and we'll talk about doing that in the next chapter.

Emotional/Mental Responses to Grief

The dark valley of grief may leave your emotions a tangled mess, sometimes nearly impossible to control and difficult to even name. Your emotions may change in an instant and without warning. You may feel things you've never felt before or be concerned because you don't feel anything like what you expected to feel.

How your emotions respond will depend a lot on your personality, the kind of relationship you had with your loved one, what kind of support you had before or have now, and more. There's no right or wrong way to feel. Others who have gone through grief have felt sadness, exhaustion, worry, fear, loneliness, panic, anger, relief, guilt, hopelessness, confusion, regret, desperation, anxiety, depression, and just about any other emotion you might name.

Anger can be an especially challenging emotion for many. You may feel angry at your loved one for leaving. You may feel angry at other family and friends for what they did, didn't do, or do or don't do now. You may feel angry at those who were involved in your loved one's care, such as medical personnel. If your loved one's death was related to addiction, murder, malpractice, or an accident or disaster, your anger may be especially marked. You may feel angry at yourself for what you did or didn't do. And you may feel angry at God for many reasons. Anger is not universal, but it's very common, and it's one of the things you will work through as you do the work of grief.

Some even feel glad after their loved one dies. If your relationship with your loved one was tumultuous, or your loved one was suffering, you may feel relieved that the person is now dead. And then you may feel guilty over feeling glad. All that is normal. You have little initial control over what emotions you feel and when.

But that doesn't mean you are completely at the mercy of your emotions. You have many choices in what you do with your feelings. This book will discuss some aspects of your grief work that will help make your emotions more manageable.

You may also experience periods—short or long—when you feel little or nothing. This can also be normal. Your mind has a number of control mechanisms that may be triggered when you experience something as overwhelmingly stressful as the death of a loved one. Those unconscious mental mechanisms may bury or short-circuit any emotions for a time. This can be a temporary blessing for some people; it gives your mind and body the opportunity to absorb what is going on and take care of other necessary matters such as working, addressing legal and practical matters around your loved one's death, caring for your children, etc.

Eventually you will need to feel those emotions. You don't have to do it all at once; indeed, you should not plan to or expect to do your emotional work quickly. But if several months have passed after your loved one's death and you are still feeling nothing, it's a sign you should seek professional help in working through your grief.

Sensing that your mind is not functioning normally is very common during grief. The enormous stress of grief biologically affects your ability to think. So much of your mind's energy is taken up with managing (or temporarily suppressing) emotions and the overwhelming "newness" of life without your loved one that there's precious little space available in your mind for clear thinking.

You may find yourself forgetting simple things, making mistakes you normally wouldn't make, feeling confused, and being unable to concentrate. Even simple choices such as whether to eat lunch or what clothes to put on may seem impossibly difficult. You may forget your loved one is dead or find yourself unable to believe he or she has passed away. Right after a loved one's death there are usually many decisions to be made, and now is exactly the time you are least able to make clear and wise decisions. If you are working, are caring for children, or have other responsibilities, those tasks may seem dramatically more difficult than usual.

You should expect the thinking and feeling parts of your mind to move much more slowly than you're used to. It's important to cut back on any responsibilities where you have the flexibility to do so. You may not be able to cut back as much as you wish, but survey your life for anything you can put on hold. Don't make any decisions you don't absolutely have to make right away. Doing your grief work over time will allow your mind to return to functioning more normally.

Grief and Relationships

Many things about your relationships will change as a result of your loved one's death. Family and friends usually come around during the early days and offer various kinds of support. Much of that is helpful; some can also feel intrusive. You need to talk about your loved one and your grief, and you also need periods alone. Many people may offer you words intended to be comforting; some will be helpful, and some, though well-intended, will feel hurtful. Give yourself permission to be with those people you find comforting and decline spending time with those you don't wish to be around, even if they don't understand your choices right now.

After the initial days are past, many of your friends and family are likely to return to their previous lives. But you are still grieving! It's usually not that others are uncaring; they didn't have the relationship with your loved one that you did. Even your closest family members, who you think should be grieving as hard as you are, are likely to respond differently than you. Understand that no one else feels exactly what you feel, and what you feel is OK.

If you had been caring for your loved one over a period, your world probably had been shrinking along with your loved one's. Now you may be left feeling like you're all alone, even though you know there are people around. The change from your intense daily involvement in caring for your loved one can leave you feeling especially unsettled when that ends. You may feel as though you don't know how to relate to people anymore. That's normal.

Many people may offer you words intended to be comforting. Give yourself permission to be with those people you find comforting and decline spending time with those you don't wish to be around.

Some friends or family may relate to you differently as well. They previously interacted with you in connection with your loved one, and they may feel unsure how to interact with you now that your loved one is not there. Some friendships may end. Some friendships or ways of relating to certain family members may change. They may be dealing with their own mixture of emotions, such as regret, guilt, sadness, confusion, anger, or relief. It may take some time for you to negotiate new ways of interacting even with family or friends you wish to stay connected to.

In some families the death of a loved one stirs up a great deal of trauma and drama. Hurt feelings lead to hurtful words, or worse. Fights over money or inheritances sometimes get ugly. Some families have secrets that come to light only after a death. The family you thought you had may look quite different now.

In other families someone's death becomes an opportunity for connection, healing, and resolution of some old wounds. Family members band together to help one another through this painful time. You cannot decide how your family will respond, but you can choose to be open to closer connections, deep conversations, and the potential for healing if other family members are also open to such. Later in this book we'll discuss some helpful ways to embrace the help others have to offer while minimizing the additional pain some relationships may bring.

Grief and Your Relationship With God

We've talked about your relationship with God already, and we will return to this topic repeatedly. But for this chapter it's important to acknowledge how grief can change and stress that relationship. Questions are normal: Why did this happen? Couldn't You have healed my loved one? Couldn't You have prevented that disaster or accident? Do You really care? Was my loved one being punished? Am I being punished now? Why did You take my loved one away? Will You take me away now too? Why don't You take this pain away? Why can't I hear or feel You when I need You so badly? Did we not have enough faith? What did I do wrong? How can You accept me when I'm feeling so angry/confused/irrational? If I trust You, why does it still hurt so bad? You seem so distant; how am I supposed to hear from You about what I'm supposed to do now?

You will probably have thoughts and questions about God, heaven, spirituality, and life that you never had before. The death of someone close to you sometimes has a way of cutting through the fog of your busy life and shining the spotlight on things you don't know, aren't sure about, have been putting off, or haven't considered. For example, if you have been part of a faith community that teaches that God's healing power is still available today, your loved one's death may challenge some things you were sure you knew about God.

Having your relationship with God challenged by grief can feel very uncomfortable. Some of the friends of God we read about in Scripture had their faith challenged in times of grief, including David (2 Sam. 12:16–23), Job (Job 1:18–21), and Mary and Martha (John 11:21–32). They didn't understand. They questioned Him. They struggled. But notice what these Bible heroes did with their questions— they presented them to God.

If these friends of God wrestled with grief, don't think it strange when you wrestle with your faith while going through the dark valley of grief. It's almost certain that your relationship with God will change as a result of this journey. As with human relationships, going through difficult things with someone changes the relationship. If you try to pretend your faith is not challenged and ignore the questions you have, you may well be surprised to find yourself shaken even more deeply in the future.

If these friends of God wrestled with grief, don't think it strange when you wrestle with your faith while going through the dark valley of grief.

This doesn't mean your relationship with God is of no benefit in the grief process. What you've learned about Him in the past will absolutely make a difference in your journey through grief. We're not talking about manufacturing questions that are not there. Some things you very well may have settled with God in the past. But it's very likely grief will find spaces in your faith you had not fully investigated. That can be a good thing. However small or large those spaces may be, don't ignore them. Ask the questions of God. He's big enough to handle them.

And if your relationship with God has been significantly unexamined, grief may make it impossible to remain where you were. You may have thought your faith was strong, and now grief has shaken that faith in ways that surprise you. If some really big questions present themselves, that's OK. Again, God's big enough to handle them.

We'll talk throughout this book about some specific steps you may find helpful in wrestling through your faith questions with and about God. Your faith *will* be different as a result of your grief journey. I'm one who can attest to the reality that your faith can become more resilient, more practically helpful, and more real as a result of this journey. But it only has the potential to become stronger if you commit to doing your grief work, including wrestling with God in whatever small or large ways your grief demands. We'll also talk about this more in later chapters.

Should a Believer Grieve?

It's unlikely a Christian will tell you outright that you should not experience grief. But it's possible for some people to express the nonverbal message that grief should not be a big deal if you're a *real* Christian. Let's set things straight. I want to again assure you that believers grieve. Job felt so depressed he wished he had never been born (Job 3:3), but he still expressed confidence that "my redeemer lives" (Job 19:25). Mary and Martha were weeping over the loss of their brother, Lazarus, even while affirming Jesus as "the Christ, the Son of God" (John 11:27, MEV). Even though these heroes did not know the resurrected Jesus, they had real faith, and they still grieved.

After Jesus' resurrection believers still grieved. Paul wrote, "But I would not have you ignorant, brothers, concerning those who are asleep, that you may not grieve as others who have no hope" (1 Thess. 4:13, MEV). Paul did not instruct the believers to refrain from grieving. As believers we are still human beings. Jesus knew that He was about to raise Lazarus from the grave, but He still wept (John 11:35). As a man Jesus felt and expressed all the emotions we are faced with, and it's OK for a believer to hurt in these ways at the death of a loved one.

Yes, our faith makes a difference. We grieve differently.

That's what this book is about. But that difference is not the absence of pain. It's a myth that believers do not or should not grieve. It's that we have something to help us through the grieving journey that others do not. And for that you and I will be forever grateful.

Goals for the Journey Through Grief

Every person's journey through grief is unique, as yours will be. But there are some goals for your journey that will be helpful to keep in mind. Knowing these goals will provide some framework for your grief work and help you see where you are making progress at times.

Accept the reality of the death.

In your humanness you have limits to what your body, mind, and soul can process in a given period. Grief is one of those experiences that overwhelms the normal mechanisms your internal system has previously relied on. Many people going through grief move back and forth between embracing the reality of their loved one's death and feeling as though it is all unreal. You may just "know" he will walk through that door any moment or expect to hear her voice when the phone rings. You may feel you are in a state of suspended animation. Your intellect may know your loved one has died, but many parts of your internal system may feel that if you just wait a little while, your loved one will be there again.

One of the goals of grief work is to come to terms with the reality of your loved one's death. As David expressed,

"Can I bring him back again? I will go to him, but he will not return to me" (2 Sam. 12:23). A funeral, memorial service, or similar event is often a way to begin this process, but for most people the process will continue for weeks, months, or even a couple of years.

Remember your loved one.

The time you had with your loved one, short or long, will always be a part of you. There were both good and difficult things that happened. Part of journeying through grief is to do the work of memory. You may want to tell stories about your loved one, listen to stories others tell about their experiences with your loved one, explore objects or digital memories related to your loved one's life, and/or create some unique and personal ways of remembering your loved one.

Many people find that intentionally doing things to remember is very helpful in the healing process. These "tasks" may trigger emotions that seems difficult to handle, but feeling those very emotions will help you move forward on your grief journey. The things you do now to remember your loved one will become even more precious as time passes.

Explore your experience of loss.

Noticing and embracing how you have responded to your loved one's death will be more helpful than you may realize. It's important to explore how your grief is impacting you physically, mentally, relationally, and spiritually. As you explore these various aspects of your experience of loss, you will understand better what you need to do moving forward.

The death of a loved one incorporates many losses. You may have lost the routine of caring for your loved one, having someone to communicate with, financial support, membership or status in certain social circles, the perspective or support or joy your loved one gave you, and much more. It's worth surveying your life for all the losses you are now faced with, acknowledging them, and choosing to give yourself grace in those areas.

Integrate your faith.

Simply applying your faith as a bandage over the wound grief has opened in your soul will not help you. Instead your faith needs to be the river into which you choose to plunge, however confusing, ever-changing, and dark it may seem. Your physical symptoms, overwhelmed emotions, mental confusion, and uncertain future need to be soaked in what you know about God and what you come to know about Him during this journey through grief. Rather than holding it as a separate "thing," your faith needs to meld with and color your pain, confusion, and uncertainty, and every aspect of the complete "newness" of your life without your loved one.

That means wrestling with God over any questions you have. It means seeking His perspective on your experience of loss and embracing whatever the journey toward healing He has for you looks like. It means searching out and experiencing how your faith and relationship with God interact with and impact all the practical aspects of daily life you are now dealing with.

Connect with others.

The wounds caused by the death of a loved one often make us want to close our souls to real connections with others. No human being will ever replace your loved one. But it will be vital for your well-being to intentionally find ways to connect with people again. I found this goal to be especially challenging and one that took a lot of emotional effort on my part. But doing so has made a big difference in coming through my own valley of grief, and it will for you also.

You will need connections with others to help you move through this dark valley, but it's more than that. The new life you are now beginning to live will need to include people—those you are able to receive something from and those to whom you give something of yourself. The previous connections you have had will be helpful but may need to be renegotiated. It's likely you also will need to make some new connections; do so slowly, in small steps. The place in your heart your loved one occupied will never be filled in the same way, but your heart and life will need people.

Choose to live.

Many who have lost a loved one initially feel that moving forward in life somehow dishonors the memory of their loved one. Choosing to remain frozen in time is a perhaps unconscious choice some people make. They stop moving and set up residence in the dark valley of grief.

While there is no medal given for speed, it is important that you keep walking. At some point you will notice the sun peeking through the clouds, and you will be offered the chance to embrace life in some way. You will feel as though you can take a breath again. Those moments will seem few and far between initially, but when they present themselves, I encourage you to say yes. Doing your memory work will help to assure your loved one will not be forgotten. And one of the best ways to honor your loved one will be to choose to go on living.

The experience of grief will impact you in many ways: physically, emotionally, relationally, and spiritually. Being unable to sleep, feeling confused, and experiencing waves of emotions without warning or the ability to control them are only some of the possible ways you will respond. Your relationships with family, friends, and God will be different as a result of this journey. What you are experiencing is unique to you, but it's almost certainly normal.

Being aware of some goals for your journey through grief can help you see where to invest the little energy you do have. A "new normal" without your loved one may seem impossible right now, but God's healing grace and your intentional grief work will make it possible. Keep walking!

TWO STEPS FORWARD

1. Think about how your body and your mind are being affected by your grief journey. Write your observations in your journal. Please be honest.

2. Think of a friend or family member you can reach out to this week just to ask him or her to support you in some way. Write that person's name in your journal and hold yourself accountable to actually call that individual.

CHAPTER 3
DOING THE NEXT THING

What wound did ever heal but by degrees?
—WILLIAM SHAKESPEARE, *OTHELLO*

WHAT DO I do now?" I would sometimes sit on my couch and ask that through my tears. The easiest response would be to do nothing. I didn't feel like doing anything. I didn't have the energy to do anything. Nothing I could do would change anything.

And yet the long list of things needing to be done seemed endless. While nothing I could do would change the reality of my husband's death, doing nothing wasn't really an option—unless I wanted to become homeless and forever dysfunctional. The only way anything would ever happen would be if I got up and did something.

Feeling overwhelmed with the physical, emotional, and spiritual responses to grief would be bad enough, but practical matters also present themselves. There's so much to do when you seem to have the fewest internal resources to do anything at all.

In this chapter we'll talk about a helpful way to go about

handling the mountain of stuff you need to do while also doing your grief work. The foundational principle is this: just do the next thing.

Looking a day, a month, or a year ahead is not something your brain can likely handle right now. Sometimes an hour is too much to think about. So just do the next thing.

Emotions and confusion seem to overwhelm your ability to plan, think, or do much at all. So just do the one next thing.

Sometimes the next thing means doing what's necessary for your survival. Sometimes it means doing your grief work. In this chapter we will explore what doing the next thing can look like.

Caring for Your Physical Health

Your body is under a lot of stress while you're grieving, and it will need some extra care during this time. Taking care of yourself in this way is not selfish or lazy. Think of it as similar to recovering after a major surgery; your body will need nutrition, rest, and exercise in order to get better. It's the same with your journey through grief.

Some have suggested the acronym DEER as a simple way to remember what your body needs:

D—Drink

E—Eat

E—Exercise

R—Rest

Sometimes doing the next thing means simply getting out of bed and putting on some clothes. Sometimes it will mean getting a drink of water. While it sounds simple, your brain will function better when you are well hydrated. Make sure you are drinking lots of water each day. It's easy to forget something so simple while you're grieving.

Sometimes doing the next thing will mean eating. A change in appetite is common during grief. You may feel unable to eat or want to constantly munch on junk food as a way to "cope." Neither is healthy. Eating some healthy food each day is often difficult for someone who is grieving, but it will be so helpful for your journey.

Make the effort to choose reasonably nutritious food. I found grocery shopping emotionally painful, and often I couldn't imagine what I could possibly want to eat. But eating healthy food is one of those "next things" that's worth putting your limited energy toward. Buy food that's easy to prepare and reasonably healthy. Consider fresh or dried fruit, yogurt, whole grain bread or crackers, or nuts. You may not feel like cooking, so look for easy-to-prepare soup or frozen meals. While limiting processed foods is generally wise, during your time of grief it's most important that you eat. Think "healthy," but prioritize getting something to eat over winning a nutrition prize.

Your body also needs to move. Grief will make you feel like sitting around and doing nothing, but some exercise will support your mental and physical well-being in many ways. If you have a porch, sit out there for a few minutes to drink your cup of coffee. Put on your shoes and take a fifteen-minute walk. Let the sunshine or the rain touch your face. Do that a couple times a day if you can. Moving, outside if possible, will improve blood flow to your brain and may even help you feel a little better in general.

One of the most surprising things in my own grief journey was how exhausted I felt. Getting rest while grieving is something many people struggle with, but it's likely you will need more than your usual amount of rest. The mental and emotional stress of the loss of your loved one drains enormous amounts of energy from your system, and you cannot recover without adequate rest.

As discussed in the last chapter, your sleep will probably be disrupted, but you are likely to feel tired. Use your body's signals to remind you to rest. That may look like a brief nap every afternoon or even a couple times during the day. If you feel able to sleep, take advantage of it. Your need for extra sleep will not last forever; it's OK to sleep whenever you're able.

To help you sleep at night, take the measures you can to prepare your mind, body, and environment for rest. Some mild exercise during the day will often help. Think about making your bedroom cool and dark. Play some calming nature sounds, white noise, or soft music if you find that relaxing. Pray specifically for God's peace and claim His promise of sleep: "In peace I will lie down and sleep, for you alone, LORD, make me dwell in safety" (Ps. 4:8).

Here's another technique you may find helpful. When preparing for bed, imagine your grief with all its pain, worry, and confusion as a "thing" that you can look at in your hands. Feel it and examine it for a few moments. Then take your grief and put it somewhere safe, such as in an imaginary box on a shelf or dresser. It will be there tomorrow morning for you to take up again. At that time, you can continue feeling what you need to feel, doing what you need to do, and going through your grief work. Don't worry if this technique doesn't work immediately or every time; it's just one additional way to help you be intentional about getting rest when you can.

Rest will be important in other ways as well. Think of some ways your mind has found refreshment in the past and do some of those things now. That might mean reading a book, sitting outside in a beautiful place in nature, listening to music, enjoying a spa, etc. Choosing some nourishment like this for your grieving soul will be helpful.

Caring for Your Mind and Emotions

Sometimes doing the next thing will mean being intentional with your grief work. That's the only way you will make progress through the dark valley of grief. Here are a few practical ways to do that.

Journal

Even if you've never journaled in the past, writing about your journey through grief may become one of the most meaningful and helpful aspects of your grief work. It doesn't have to be fancy or follow a specific format. You may wish to obtain a special journal to write about your loved one and your journey, but what's important is that you just begin. Even if you start with just a few sentences, the process will almost certainly become one of the "next things" that you will end up treasuring.

What do you write? Anything can be helpful. Write about your loved one, about how you are responding to his or her death, and what your thoughts and feelings are now. If you need some ideas on what to write about, consider writing a letter to your loved one or writing a letter to Jesus about what you're feeling. You can also use the following questions as writing prompts.

- What did your loved one mean to you? What was special about the person as an individual?

- What do you miss right now about your loved one?

- What would you like to tell your loved one if you could do so?

- What reminded you of your loved one today? How did it feel?

- What worries you about the future? What challenges are you facing as a result of your loved one's death?

- What about your loved one's life do you want to carry with you into the future?

- How did your loved one impact who you are as a person?

- Has God been saying anything to you through your grief journey?

When a wave of emotion overwhelms you, make journaling one of your "go to" things to do. Writing about what you feel and about what triggered those feelings can be an important way to both embrace and work through your feelings. It can also be a helpful way to bring God's perspective to your grief journey. Write out the questions you have for Him. Write anything you may hear Him saying to you. Write about what you are learning. You may be surprised how helpful this tool can become.

Remember.

There are many ways to remember your loved one. Spending a portion of your time and energy in remembering will be a helpful way to work through your emotions and thoughts.

During the initial days after your loved one's death you may have received many messages from friends and family expressing what your loved one meant to them and how much they care about you. Read those messages again—the ones on social media, in the cards or letters you received, or on the online obituary page for your loved one. You may wish to look at pictures or listen to recordings from your loved one's funeral or memorial service. Those can become precious times.

You may wish to create some physical ways to remember your loved one. I made a shadow box of items from my husband's funeral and had a memory quilt made from a number of his favorite shirts and jackets. There are many other creative options to remember your loved one. You may not feel able to do something like this right away; that's one of the important reasons not to get rid of your loved one's personal effects until you feel ready. Going through his or her belongings can be a treasure trove of help in your grief work. We'll talk more about this in chapter 6.

Visiting your loved one's resting place is very meaningful for some and not helpful at all for others. There's no right or wrong frequency of visiting, and some people never do so. For some the grave site can be a place to say things to their loved one as a way of working through thoughts and feelings, and at times they experience God's presence in a very healing way. If circumstances prevented you from having a resting place for your loved one, you may wish to choose a special place to remember him or her anyway, such as somewhere in nature or a lovely chapel your loved one enjoyed.

Remembering cannot be done all at once. It's one of the "next things" to regularly return to as you walk this journey through grief.

Address legal or business matters.

Frequently a loved one's death will result in a multitude of financial, business, and/or legal matters that must be addressed. We'll talk more about this in chapter 6, but for now just know that sometimes doing the next thing means making progress in these practical areas.

Your next thing today might be making a list of the

organizations you need to contact, asking a friend for a referral to an attorney, making a single phone call, or taking some other small action in relation to a practical matter. These practical matters may feel overwhelming or confusing, and you shouldn't expect to be able to handle them all at once or quickly. The important thing is to just do one small "next thing" when you can.

It bears repeating that, if possible, it's wise to delay any big decisions, perhaps for six months or a year. There will be plenty of matters that cannot be delayed, but put off what you can. If you don't absolutely have to move or change jobs, for example, don't. There will be many "next things" to handle in the meantime.

Take time to feel.

Sometimes you need to take a break simply to allow a feeling to run its course. A wave of sadness, anger, frustration, or some other emotion will come, and you will need to find a safe place to let it wash over you. Trying to stuff those emotional waves underground will take even more of your precious energy and end up sabotaging your journey through grief. And the feelings you deny or refuse to experience today have real potential to become destructive in the future.

An emotional wave may come when you least expect it— at the grocery store, at work, while you are with friends, at church, or wherever. If possible, allow yourself to experience that wave right away. If alone, just pause what you're doing and feel it. If you're with someone safe, you may wish to talk about it. If you're with others and can excuse yourself to step outside or go to the bathroom for a moment, that may help.

Sometimes these emotional waves come when you can't excuse yourself, such as when you're at work or doing something important with your children. Acknowledge to yourself what you have felt, and give yourself some grace. Then it's important to return to that emotional place later when you have some space to deal with it. Intentionally doing some grief work at least several times a week will help you regain some sense of mastery over your emotions. Trust that you won't always feel as out of control as you do now.

Do nothing.

It's likely you will feel significantly energy-depleted as you journey through grief. As when recovering from some serious illness or surgery, your system will not be able to do things at the pace you're used to. Even if you are trying to be intentional about using your energy wisely, you may find yourself unable to spend more than a few hours a day doing "next things." Your brain does not have the capacity to process grief twenty-four hours a day. It's perfectly normal and healthy to have times when you do nothing. Vegging out in front of the TV or doing something similar may be an OK distraction from your uncertain feelings and tumultuous thoughts.

Simply finding distraction and doing nothing can be a necessary part of your grief process. Just make certain you don't fall into the trap of *only* distracting yourself. If you are doing some grief work several times a week, you are probably doing what you need to do. Some type of distraction or entertainment, or simply sitting and doing nothing, may be the only "next thing" you can do the rest of the time. Remember, there are no medals for speed in this journey.

Seek God's comfort.

Among the "next things" you will need to do is seek and embrace God's comfort. You would not have picked up this book if you didn't believe God is somehow involved in this whole thing about life and death. At times, it may be very difficult to hear His voice or feel His presence. The emotions of grief can be like clouds that cover the sun; He hasn't gone away, but your ability to see or hear Him can be obscured by grief. That's only human.

God will not try to hurry you up just to make you feel better. He respects your humanness and limitations, and He understands them even better than you do. But you can be assured from the Bible and from the testimony of countless others who have experienced grief before you that He is still there. He's not overwhelmed by your emotions, confusion, questions, or anger. He isn't

> **God isn't overwhelmed by your emotions, confusion, questions, or anger. He isn't going anywhere, and He'll be as patient as you need Him to be in walking this journey with you.**

going anywhere, and He'll be as patient as you need Him to be in walking this journey with you.

Your journey through grief can be smoothed, softened, and shortened by intentionally taking steps to connect with God and the comfort He offers. This is different from sitting back and waiting for God to magically make your pain go away. Remember that healing and comfort are things you choose. It's like food. God puts fish in the sea, but He doesn't put them on your plate or in your mouth. He makes the grain grow, but He doesn't bake your bread or hand you a sandwich. Healing and comfort are available, but you must intentionally seek them.

Here are some ways to seek and embrace God's comfort in this process.

Read God's Word.

Your mind may struggle to focus on reading the Bible even if that has been a part of your routine in the past. That's OK. Use this season to look at what God has to say about the very things you are wrestling with. A few verses a day may be all your mind can take in, but that will be like superfood to your soul if you do it regularly.

There are devotional books and email series for people going through grief. That may be a great resource for you to assist in taking God's Word into your being daily. I encourage you to also do some Bible reading on your own. Here are a few passages you may find especially helpful during this time.

- Psalm 90, Moses' prayer about God's constancy and man's frailty

- John 11, the story of Jesus, Mary, Martha, and Lazarus

- First Corinthians 15, Paul's treatise on death and resurrection

So many of the psalms express honest human emotion in prayer to God, emotions such as fear, grief, hopelessness, feeling overwhelmed, frustration, confusion, anger, and pain as well as hope and faith. If you can't do anything else, open to Psalms and read a few verses. See if you don't soon find your own thoughts and feelings expressed. You may want to use a psalm as your own prayer to God.

Talk to God.

Prayer is like breathing. You can't survive without it. Many believers find prayer challenging during the journey through grief. You may not know what to say, or you may struggle with believing God hears you. That's normal.

More than any other "next thing," please just pray. That may be nothing more than a word or two: "God, help me! I'm drowning!" Or, "What do I do now?" Or, "I don't like this!" It may be a silent "Jesus!" through your tears or frustration. Just do it. Direct your mind and words to God. When you can cry out, do it. Prayer may look different during your process of grief than it does at other times. What makes it prayer is that you point your soul in God's direction and reach out to Him. Sometimes tears are your prayer if they're pointed in His direction.

And as often as you can, stay there. Don't rush out of His presence. Be your real, confused, tired, broken, angry, hurting, or overwhelmed self with Him. Sometimes try to imagine Him there with you. This is such an important step that we'll mention it in several different contexts throughout this book.

It's usually in those quiet moments in God's presence, when your own emotions have played themselves out and you are still, that He will minister to your heart. It's in those moments when He will say, "I'm here." You won't feel, see, or hear Him the same way every time. Sometimes your humanness may not feel Him there at all. But stick around. That's part of putting yourself in the position to receive His healing and comfort. You can be certain that He will meet you there if you keep coming back.

Find what helps you connect with Him.

There are other ways many people have found meaningful in connecting with God during their grief process. Worship music can open doors to the soul that are sometimes hard to open any other way. You can listen to worship music while alone, while doing other activities, and in corporate gatherings. Try listening to music, and see if there aren't places in your soul that open up.

Being around God's creation can minister peace and healing in meaningful ways, and it's often where grieving people hear His voice. One of the most meaningful times I had with God in my own journey through grief was a very long walk along the beach where He ministered deeply to my heart. Find places in nature that are enjoyable to you. Watch the squirrels play or listen to the birds sing. Walk slowly through a garden or along a creek. Take a really long look at the stars at night. God's creation is where you may meet Him.

Being around other believers will also be important. You may not feel able to engage in church the way you're used to, or perhaps you haven't gone in some time. Make an effort to go now when you can. It's OK to sit in the back alone if you wish, or to ask a friend to go with you and just sit beside you quietly. Being in the company of other believers can allow their faith to rub off on you a bit, and it will help you choose healing and comfort. And if you get emotional in church, that's just fine. It's part of the journey.

During your time of grief it will seem as though there are so many things to do at the very time you have so little energy and capacity for doing anything. Don't try to do everything. Just do the next thing.

Those "next things" will include taking care of your body with nutrition and rest. It will include doing your grief work such as journaling, remembering, and giving space to your emotions. It must also include intentionally seeking connection with God on a daily basis, as difficult as that sometimes seems.

As you do these "next things" regularly, a few of them

each day, you will be making progress. Periodically you will realize that you've moved a little further along on the journey. And when you notice that, pause for a moment of gratitude. The dark valley will have an end.

TWO STEPS FORWARD

1. How are you doing with DEER: drinking, eating, exercising, and resting? Which one do you need to gently encourage yourself to do more consistently? Write in your journal about some way in which you will take care of yourself regularly.

2. Are you allowing yourself some specific times to feel and remember each week? If not, when will you do that in the next few days?

CHAPTER 4
HEALTHY AND UNHEALTHY GRIEVING

And we wept that one so lovely should have a life so brief.
—WILLIAM CULLEN BRYANT, "THE DEATH OF THE FLOWERS"

JUST MAKE THE pain go away!" For one who is grieving, that's usually one of the deepest heart cries. Death hurts! If it weren't so painful, perhaps we could handle it better. Intellectually you may know that experiencing pain at the death of a loved one is expected. But when it hurts *so bad*, it's only human to try to do whatever you can to ease the pain.

Thankfully the human mind is amazingly resilient, and there are many ways of easing the pain of grief. Some of these strategies actually help you move along in your journey through this valley. Others, however, short-circuit, sabotage, or delay your journey and have the potential to only deepen your pain in the future.

There's no "right" way to grieve. There's no checklist or rule book or treatment plan that you can follow. (How I wished for such a checklist during the early days of my own grief!) But understanding some of the ways people have responded to grief can help you focus your own responses in a more fruitful and constructive direction. For lack of a better way to describe them, we'll call these responses to grief healthy and unhealthy. Here's what they look like.

Unhealthy Ways of Responding to Grief

Think of unhealthy responses to grief as setting up residence in the dark valley. Many of these unhealthy responses are ways people seek to numb the pain that comes with grief, but all of them in some way keep you stuck where you are.

It's been said that if you're in a valley, a pit, a mess, don't stay there; keep going! Unhealthy responses to grief keep you stuck in the mire without moving you forward. The following are some possible responses to grief you will want to avoid.

Isolating yourself

When humans are hurt, one of the most natural responses is to try to hide. It's as if you physically and/or emotionally curl up into a ball, wrap your tail around your face, and close yourself off to the outside world. You refuse to accept that anyone or anything outside yourself could be useful, and you rebuff any attempts from others to connect with you.

Rest and significant times of solitude are vital for your grief journey, but when being alone turns into isolation, it becomes destructive. Your personality will impact how big of a trap isolation is for you, but anyone going through grief is tempted to isolate. It just hurts so much you feel like turning into yourself and nursing your wounds. Turning inward seems the safest option, but it actually prevents helpful input and keeps you stuck in the worst part of your pain.

Your grief is your own; no other human being can understand every aspect of what you're going through. But you do need people. How do you know if you're isolating? Ask yourself if you are letting other people in and if you're letting God in. Other people cannot do your grieving for you or take your pain away, but it's vital that you allow both human and divine input and connection.

Turning inward seems the safest option, but it actually prevents helpful input and keeps you stuck in the worst part of your pain.

I believe every grieving person needs human contact several times each week. Sometimes that human contact may be somewhat superficial, such as sitting in church while silently weeping and saying nothing. Sometimes that human contact should be more "real," such as attending a grief support group and sharing a little of your pain. This will be easier for some than others. If you're the kind of person who tends to isolate, you may need to expend more than the usual amount of energy in choosing human connections. We'll talk more about this in chapter 5.

Abusing substances

I never knew my father-in-law, but he did not respond to his wife's death in a healthy way. My husband told me that from shortly after her funeral until his death a few years later his father was rarely sober. Although it wasn't immediate, he literally drank himself to death.

For someone prone to addiction, using alcohol, illegal drugs, or pills to numb out after a loved one's death may seem the "natural" way to dull the pain. It's an understandable response, but it always leads to destruction. You might think this would not be a likely trap for believers, but that's not necessarily so. Your defenses are down when you're faced with the overwhelming pain of grief, and using some substance to dull the pain or go to sleep can seem an easier way out than wrestling with the feelings involved.

I believe people who are still processing the loss of a loved one should not use any substance of any kind on their own to dull the pain of grief. The dangers are too great. It may be difficult to find healthier ways to soothe your emotions, but it's worth the slow and painful effort to do so. This is where doing your grief work comes in.

You may be wondering, "What about prescription medications such as antidepressants or sleeping pills?" This is not an easy question to answer, primarily because our culture desires instant gratification. The thinking seems to be, if you don't feel good, look to a pill to fix you. Some doctors have fallen into this pattern as well, knowing that a prescription is one of the few things they have to offer that might help someone feel better, even if only temporarily.

If you are stuck in grief and unable to function, there are times when it is necessary and appropriate to use prescription medication under the close supervision of your doctor. Look at such medication not as a way to be fixed but as one tool to help you function while you are doing the other parts of your grief work.

Engaging in excessive activity

Throwing yourself into constant activity can be a means of delaying your grief work. That may look like long hours at work, lots of travel, or other significant projects. Getting involved in life and activities again can be a healthy way of dealing with grief *unless* you are using such activity as a way to avoid exploring your feelings and doing your grief work.

No one can tell you how much time you should spend feeling bad or how much energy you must devote specifically to grief work. But if you are using the activities you choose to engage in as a way of totally eclipsing your mind and emotions to the point that you are numbing your feelings, that's not healthy.

The danger here is that your grief goes underground. You are only pretending that you're not in a dark valley. Sometime later the thoughts and feelings you are not dealing with will certainly come out in destructive ways. That may look like a rebound romantic relationship after losing a spouse, irritable and angry ways of treating others at work, or a completely out-of-proportion response to some comparatively minor stress down the road.

Take the time now to deal with your grief. Do your grief work. It's the only way to get through the valley of grief.

Wallowing

At the opposite extreme from excessive activity is wallowing in grief. If you tend to respond this way, you may feel as though you have no reason to go on living without your loved one. You spend every moment of every day grieving—crying, thinking and talking about your loved one, reliving moments with your loved one, spending long hours at your loved one's resting place, investing money you don't have in memorials, etc.

All these things are part of healthy grieving: crying, remembering your loved one, talking about him or her, visiting the person's resting place, etc. It only becomes wallowing when that's all you are doing, and you are investing no energy in moving forward. No one can tell you how quickly you will or should move through the dark valley of grief, but it's important that you choose to take steps that move you forward.

How do you know if you're wallowing? Ask yourself if you are choosing healing. You won't feel like you're on a healing journey every day. Some days will be very difficult, and you won't always feel like choosing healing. That's OK. But are you taking a step forward? Are you spending bits of time with people who are uplifting and positive? Are you seeking God's perspective on your grief and asking for His guidance for the next phase of your life? If the answers to those questions are yes, you're probably not wallowing.

Numbing out

Grief hurts. And besides excessive activity or substance abuse there are plenty of other ways to numb out. That might be vegging out in front of the TV for endless hours, sleeping away both your days and nights, compulsive shopping, playing video games, or anything else to keep your mind occupied and distracted.

The only way to get through the pain is to feel it. You can't concentrate on the full weight of your grief every moment of every day, and you need definite times of distraction, rest, even entertainment. Again, no one can tell you how much time to spend doing your grief work. Your mind and emotions have a finite amount of energy with which to engage in your grief work, and periods of numbing out aren't wrong in themselves (as long as the activity is not in itself destructive).

The point is to make sure you are taking a small step forward on a regular basis. Are you allowing yourself periods of time to feel emotions? Are you choosing to do some grief work at least a few times each week? Are you taking steps to regularly connect with God along the way? If so, you're probably doing fine. It's super hard to look days, weeks, or months into the future when you're grieving, and you don't have to. But keep choosing to take one small step forward at a time.

Healthy Ways of Responding to Grief

Some of the healthy responses to grief we already mentioned in the last chapter. I'll elaborate on a few of them and add some others. These are ways of responding to grief that actually help you move forward through the dark valley instead of setting up residence there.

These responses are most important in the first weeks and months after the death of your loved one, but most grieving people will need to continue these in some measure for a much longer time. Many significant elements of grief last two or three years for many, if not most, people. The unhealthy ways of responding to grief can delay your healing process, but even these healthier ways of responding may not make your grieving process much shorter. These healthier ways of responding will help you be more functional right from the start, bring you more healing, and do much to help you discover what God has next for you. But this will still take time.

There are also some very real aspects of grief that never go away. That may sound discouraging, but it's really not. Remembering your loved one will always be important, but the sting of that memory can be healed over time. You may always have times when difficult feelings around your loved one wash over you, but the disruptiveness of those feelings can definitely lessen. The aspects of grief you continue to carry with you will become softer over time and can actually become very precious.

Part of the journey through grief is learning new ways of thinking, behaving, believing, connecting, doing life, and trusting God. These healthier ways of responding to grief are part of developing these new ways of being. You are carrying your loved one with you, though you are having to learn to live without that person's physical presence. These elements will not only be valuable during the initial months after your loved one's death but also will help you develop patterns that will serve you well even much later.

Making space for your feelings

There are innumerable things that may trigger various emotions around the loss of your loved one. Those triggers will not always be as powerful as they are right now, but they will not completely go away. That's actually a good thing. When those feelings come, you are reminded of what your loved one meant to you and who you are as a result of your relationship with that person. It's part of who you are.

When a feeling such as sadness, loneliness, anger, fear, worry, pain, regret, etc. washes over you, learn to experience it as a wave. It will rise in intensity, reach a peak, and then lessen. Ignoring the wave doesn't make it go away. Often the best response is to ride the wave. During the early periods after your loved one's death these waves will feel unmanageable. As you learn to ride the wave, you will come to feel less out of control. Learn to recognize your feelings as real and also acknowledge that your feelings do not constitute the whole truth.

You can choose some things in advance that you will do when those feelings come. That may look like stopping what you're doing and focusing on the wave, crying if you must for a few moments, etc. If necessary, you can let others around you know you just need a moment alone. That can also look like breathing out a prayer to God, taking a moment to remember your loved one, or choosing a verse, poem, or saying to think about.

The important thing is to acknowledge and own your feelings while not allowing them to be your master. That will become easier over time, especially if you intentionally think in these ways while doing your grief work.

Guarding your physical health

The impact of grief on your physical health is real, and it's important you give your body some extra TLC during this time. As mentioned previously, that starts with drinking, eating, exercising, and resting appropriately. It's likely your patterns for even these basic lifestyle necessities will be altered; be intentional about addressing these fundamentals of self-care.

Sometimes the physical symptoms you experience may indicate a more serious health condition. You may have also put off regular medical care for yourself, especially if you were heavily involved in caring for your loved one. And the stress of grief may uncover some health concerns you were more easily able to ignore in the past.

For these reasons and more, it's helpful to get a medical evaluation some time during the early months after your loved one's death, more quickly if you're having worrisome symptoms. With so much of your emotions and thinking taken up with grief-related things, it may be harder than normal for you to determine what's serious and what's not.

A doctor's checkup will reassure you if there's nothing to worry about and prompt you to get some help if there is.

Doing one thing at a time

Trying to get everything done quickly or not taking any steps at all to "take care of business" are two ways to make your grief process harder than it needs to be. As previously mentioned, the healthiest way to go about taking care of the many things you need to do is slowly and steadily. That includes the practical matters such as legal or financial issues or dealing with your loved one's belongings. It applies just as much to your more direct grief work, such as journaling, remembering, working through your emotions, or wrestling with God about questions you have.

Get into a pattern of dealing with one thing at a time as much as possible. That's really all your mind will be able to focus on anyway. For today that might mean one phone call, going through one drawer, making one journal entry, or making one small decision. It may be very difficult to look further ahead than today or this week; that's OK. That's why taking small steps one at a time is all you should worry about.

Taking actions or making decisions that involve months or years in the future is usually unwise during the first year after a loved one's death. Postpone big decisions for six to twelve months whenever possible, and if you can't, look for someone to help you think through that decision. As time goes by, your ability to think about longer-time horizons will improve. Right now just do the next thing for today and then stop until tomorrow.

Embracing the memories

This is related to making space for your feelings and doing the next thing, but it deserves specific mention. As I said in an earlier chapter, remembering your loved one and doing things in response is an important part of healthy grieving. Trying to not remember is an underlying issue in several of the unhealthy responses to grief mentioned previously.

Tell stories about your loved one. Don't be afraid to mention him or her to others, and ask what they remember as well. Write about or to your loved one. Take your time in going through his or her belongings. You may also want to create physical reminders of your loved one's life and who he or she was to you. All those things can be meaningful and healing in your journey.

Accepting help

Times of solitude are healthy and necessary; isolation is not. Accepting help is an important part of grieving in a healthy way. Our culture today makes this more difficult than it perhaps was in the past when extended family and close-knit communities did life together over many years. But there are many ways in which help is available. It's OK to lean on others during this season more than you normally would.

While others cannot understand everything about your experience, your family and friends likely want to be supportive. Let them help you. Reach out for practical help if you need to. Get professional help if you're not coping. (We'll talk more about this in chapter 5.) It's OK to just call a friend or family member and ask that person to listen. As I mentioned before, if there are significant decisions you are not able to delay, ask someone you trust to talk through the decision with you.

It's also healthy to connect with others who have lost loved ones. Your church may offer such a program. Hospice organizations or funeral homes often offer such support, or they can refer you to such a program in your community. Taking advantage of such support may feel awkward at first, but you are likely to find it helpful.

Finding comfort

Comfort may seem elusive during the early days and weeks of your grief journey. It can be helpful to intentionally look for healthy ways to find comfort. Your personality and your history with your loved one will color what this looks like for you individually. Try to imagine moments when you felt calm and peaceful in the past, and see if there are small things from those previous experiences that you can bring into your experience now as a way to find moments of comfort.

That might look like lighting a candle, soaking in a bubble bath, sitting outside and listening to the birds sing, holding a piece of your loved one's clothing, enjoying a favorite cup of tea, or listening to some of your favorite music. Look for those sensory moments that calm and nourish your body and soul, and intentionally let your heart feel comforted. Your pain will not go away; indeed, looking for comfort may well bring on tears. But investing moments of time and energy in embracing comfort will help sustain you through this dark valley. (Just make sure you are not using the unhealthy grieving methods mentioned earlier.)

Taking God with you on the journey

I've said it before, but it bears repeating: reaching out for God's perspective and support is one of the most important aspects of grieving in a healthy way. You may have periods when your faith seems relatively strong and you know God will be with you through this journey. Then the very next day or week things may seem unusually dark, and you may feel like God is distant and uninvolved. Remember that it's you who is changing, not God. It's OK to go through these different emotional states when it comes to your connection with God. The important thing is to keep choosing to pursue a relationship with Him.

A healthy habit to get into is to direct your thoughts, emotions, and questions to God regardless of how small or large they seem. He's there with you twenty-four hours a day, and you can be sure you're not bothering Him. You can do this dozens of times a day if need be.

If you're lying awake at night, ask God to bless you with restful sleep. If you're confused and don't know what to do next, reach out with a "Lord, what do I do now?" When you feel lonely, say, "Jesus, are You here with me?" When you're angry, cry out, "Why did this have to happen?"

When you feel as though you have no reason to go on, say, "Jesus, I need You to give me a purpose, even for just today." When you don't know who to reach out to, ask, "Lord, who are You sending me that I need to connect with?" Do life with Jesus moment by moment.

Will that magically make everything OK? It won't feel OK. You won't always hear or feel an immediate, intellectually satisfying answer. But going through this grief process with God will become one of the truly meaningful aspects of your entire relationship with Him. Your sense of trust in Him and ability to hear His voice will increase as a result.

Does that sound too "spiritual" and too hard? It's not. Whatever relationship with God you had in the past will be stretched through your grief journey, and that's a good thing. In the places where it was strong, your faith will be a support, but your previous faith will not be completely enough to rest on. You will need to consciously choose to exercise your faith and connect with God as you move forward. That may feel messy and uncertain, but it will be one of the most important parts of choosing and experiencing healing.

The pain of grief will demand that you respond in some way. You can't not respond. How you respond will either move you forward through the dark valley of grief or sabotage and delay your journey.

Unhealthy responses to grief may seem like the only ways available to deal with overwhelming pain, but they actually lead you to take up residence in the dark valley. These unhealthy responses include isolation, substance abuse, excessive activity, wallowing, and numbing out. Anything that prevents you from regularly doing your grief work can end up causing more pain in the end.

Healthy responses to grief help move you forward on your journey, even though you may progress slowly and with difficulty. Healthy responses include creating space for your feelings, caring for your physical body, accepting help, remembering, doing the next thing, and taking God with you on the journey. It may not immediately feel like it, but these activities will truly help you move out of the worst of your pain.

TWO STEPS FORWARD

1. Did you see yourself in any of the examples of unhealthy ways of grieving? While still being gentle with yourself, are there any steps you could take to do things differently?

2. How are you seeking comfort? Are you seeking comfort from God? Why or why not?

CHAPTER 5
DO NOT GRIEVE ALONE

'I would rather walk with a friend in the
dark than walk alone in the light.
—Helen Keller

For millennia human beings have recognized the importance of grieving together. Many of the rituals surrounding death in various cultures involve the community coming together to support those who lost a loved one. In Scripture the children of Israel mourned important deaths for many days. Deuteronomy 34:8 says the Israelites mourned Moses' death for thirty days. In some communities widows have worn only black for a full year, in part to give those around her the opportunity to continue offering support.

Our mobile, modern culture has lost something in the way we individualize grief. The funeral or memorial service brings others together to support those who have lost a loved one, and that can be a pivotal time in the grieving process. But that is only one moment. In our fast-moving society most of those present initially will soon go about their own lives, often causing the grieving person to feel alone.

Pain is a very private thing in itself, but that doesn't mean you need to or should carry it alone. Today many of us aren't part of an extended family or close-knit community that will automatically stick with us through a long and challenging grieving process. That means you will need to be a little more intentional about connecting with others.

Some people find it difficult to admit how much they need others, especially during a season as challenging as grief. Finding ways to connect doesn't usually happen without some intentional actions on your part. In this chapter we will look at some healthy ways to develop a network of people who will walk alongside you on this journey.

Why Connecting Is Hard

The private nature of pain makes most of us want to hide—from ourselves, from others, or even from God. Grief makes us feel raw and vulnerable, and we don't want to be hurt even more. You've probably already had positive and negative experiences in connecting with others, both in your current grief journey and in the past. Even well-meaning friends and family can say or do things that end up causing you pain. Feeling reluctant to connect is normal.

Your world also may have gotten smaller recently, especially if you were deeply involved in taking care of your loved one prior to the person's death. Caretaking is a tough journey in itself. As loved ones move closer to death, their world shrinks, and it's hard for their caretakers' world not to shrink too. Even though it's important for caretakers to stay connected to others, it can be a real challenge.

I faced that problem personally. My husband was becoming increasingly ill just when we moved to a new city. We initially attempted to connect to a new church and find local friends in our new neighborhood, but his physical limitations made that very difficult. I realized after his death that I had no close friends nearby who could go through this journey with me. I appreciated family, but they were grieving also. It took a great deal of the energy I did have to intentionally make real, new connections with people. Though challenging, my efforts to make real connections with new friends and a church fellowship have helped my grief process and provided a lot of meaning for my new season of life. If you do have close friends, reach out to them now. But if you find yourself grieving without the support of a close community, as I once did, now is the time to use a portion of your energy to reach out.

> **Others cannot grieve for you, but you need them. It isn't healthy to grieve completely alone.**

However easy or hard connecting is for you, it's vital. Others cannot grieve for you, but you need them. It isn't healthy to grieve completely alone.

What You *Can* and *Cannot* Expect From Others

No one can take away your pain. You may want friends or loved ones to, and they may want to, but it's not in their power to do so. They cannot fix you, answer all your questions, or be there every moment when you feel upset. They cannot make you choose healing or do your grief work for you. They cannot make decisions for you or tell you what you're supposed to do next. As much as you might wish for others to do some of these things, you cannot outsource the grieving process. This is a journey you must take yourself.

That may sound disappointing or even downright depressing, but with each step you take, you will gain strength and perspective, and find healing. Fortunately, you don't have to—and shouldn't—take the journey alone. You must move your own legs, but you should do so alongside others. You'll want to be intentional about staying close enough to others so that when you stumble, someone is there to support you. Choose to open bits of your heart to caring people, even if it's for short amounts of time. Although you're the one doing the walking through this dark valley, you can choose to place yourself close enough to others for someone to hear you when you call out in need.

There are many things others can do to support you on your journey. Choosing to connect may take you out of your comfort zone, but it's worth it. There are likely people you already know whom you can ask to listen or assist in other ways. There are also individuals you perhaps don't know yet whom you can also reach out to. Here are some ways in which others can help.

Listening

You don't need a listening ear 24/7, but you do need to talk. You need to tell stories about your loved one and share what this grieving process is like for you. Talking can become an important way to work through feelings, remember your loved one, make decisions, feel support, and get perspective on your relationship with God. Having a few people in your life who can listen will be so helpful.

If you don't have someone in your life who already fills this role, reach out. Ask a colleague at work or someone you know at church, "If I need to talk, can I call you or meet for coffee?" Many reasonable people would be happy to say yes. You are giving your friends a gift by trusting them to listen. Let them know you're not asking for advice, just a listening ear.

This is one of the many benefits of a small group also, whether it's one for people who have lost a loved one or some other kind of group. Simply talking about your loved one and how you are experiencing grief will be more helpful than you can imagine, and it may even be comforting.

Offering practical help

People may have already said to you, "Call if you need anything." And most of us never call. God bless that friend or family member who doesn't wait for you to call but simply reaches out with some specific help! That doesn't happen to all of us, so it's important to know that it's OK for you to ask for help.

If you have children you're responsible for, ask a trusted

friend or neighbor to watch them for an hour or two so you can take care of other matters or just think. If you lost a spouse who used to take care of some practical matters around the home, ask someone for help if you need it. If you don't know where to go for some legal or business advice, ask someone for a suggestion or referral.

One practical note: don't ask someone to go through your loved one's personal belongings for you. As difficult as that task may be, it's too important a part of your grief journey to delegate to others. Perhaps not today, but the time will come when you will be grateful you did this task yourself.

Giving wisdom or perspective

Chances are you will be faced with philosophical or other big life questions during your grief journey. You may also face some decisions that are larger than you feel able to adequately think through on your own. Sometimes you need a guide or counselor to help along the way.

You may already know a pastor, church leader, wise friend, or "mother" or "father" in the Lord who would be happy to give you some perspective. It's a mark of wisdom on your part to know that you need some outside help. Don't hesitate to ask for it. I did on more than one occasion, and it made a big difference in helping me move forward on my journey.

Sometimes that help can best be provided by a professional. Some pastors, for example, have training in helping people along the grief process. If you're struggling greatly and making no progress on your own, prayerfully consider seeing a professional counselor, therapist, pastor, or psychologist who has special training and experience in helping people through grief. Not all pastors have this kind of training or experience, but your church may be able to suggest an appropriate professional. You can also ask your funeral director or people you know who have gone through their own grief journey for referrals. Get some help if you need it.

Providing companionship

I'm not talking about romantic relationships here at all. I'm talking about finding others who have lost a loved one, fellow travelers on the grief journey. You may be surprised how validating and helpful it can be to connect with others who are grieving. While your experience is completely unique, being in a place to mutually share one another's struggles during the grief journey can be comforting and supportive.

If you're struggling greatly and making no progress on your own, prayerfully consider seeing someone who has special training in helping people through grief.

Good places to look for this kind of companionship include your church and hospices in your community. Hospice grief groups are usually open to those who have lost loved ones even if that loved one was not a hospice patient. Visit a group for a couple weeks. If it doesn't seem to fit your needs, check out another.

Funeral home directors also can be good resources for finding grief groups.

At unexpected times you may meet others who are grieving. These companions in the journey may become especially valuable because many of your previous relationships will change. You and someone else experiencing grief will be able to understand each other in ways that even the most caring friend who has not experienced grief will be unable to. Some of these companions may play a very limited role. I met a woman who had lost her husband a couple years before Al died, and meeting with her for lunch on occasion gave me an opportunity to share about my grief. But she had a tendency to talk incessantly about herself, so I limited my contact with her. Other companions will be more meaningful. A new church acquaintance had also lost her husband, and she and I have been able to support each other repeatedly in many ways. Remain open to the new companions God will bring you along this journey.

Relationship Challenges During Grief

Your relationships with the people in your life will change after you have lost a loved one. Some people will struggle to know how to relate to you without your loved one. Others may be so absorbed in their own lives that they don't have the emotional space to connect during your loss. Some friendships may end. Some of these changes may be painful, but some of them may also be helpful. You will also find opportunities to form new relationships.

Here are some ways to address specific challenges you may face in various types of relationships.

Family members

Family are usually the ones who knew your loved one the best (perhaps besides you), and they may well be grieving also. We all grieve in our own unique way. Don't assume your family members didn't love or care for your loved one because they aren't grieving in the same way you are. Even if the relationship seems similar, such as a mother and father grieving the death of a child or two siblings grieving the death of a parent, personalities are different. Your relationships with the loved one who died were different. Your grieving process is different, and the kind of healing you need is different. You may need to give your family members some grace in this area.

Sometimes a death in the family brings skeletons out of the closet. Painful secrets may now be out in the open. Some family relationships may have been held together by the loved one who died, and certain family members may now feel free to put their underlying anger, jealousy, or other issues on full display. While this can make the grieving process feel even more disruptive, it also provides you an opportunity to deal with the truth in a way you may not have before.

You may not wish to spend much time with certain family members during your time of grief. Some family members may say things or respond in ways that make you feel angry, hurt, or upset. Remember this truth: it's OK to say no. It's OK to limit your time with certain people if you don't want to be with them, and you don't owe them a detailed explanation. If you feel obligated to explain, make it very brief: "I'm dealing with some important things in my personal grief process right now, and I'll be better able to talk another time."

You may also wish certain family members or friends would understand specific things about your experience or support you in particular ways. Consider writing a grief letter to these important family members or close friends. Writing can allow you time to think through what you feel and need. When you're comfortable with the letter, give it to your family member or friend with a comment such as, "Here are a few things I'd like you to know, and I found writing an easier way to say it clearly."

Remember, a time will come when you will be facing your own death. The people most likely to surround you at that time will be your loved ones. Be willing to renegotiate your relationships with family members if necessary, but continue to invest in them whenever it is possible.

Friends

Thank God for faithful friends! If you have one or a few friends who are close to you, this may be the time their friendship becomes more valuable than ever. Although they probably knew your loved one, they are not likely to be affected as deeply as you are by the person's death. A friend may often have more energy than family members to be supportive during this time. Welcome that support.

Some friends, however, may withdraw. This can feel like rubbing salt in an open wound; they disappear at just the time you need them most. It's not likely a wise use of your precious energy to go chasing after them. Yes, reach out. But if it's clear they are moving in a different direction, use your energy elsewhere. Some friends may struggle in relating to you without your loved one, or they may have other emotional limitations. Some friendships may be rescued by having an open conversation. You can say something like, "I know my loved one is not here, and I know it feels awkward. But I value you. I need you. Can we stay connected?" Welcome those friends who have something to offer, and accept that some friends may not have what you need.

Many people going through grief feel lonely and that no one understands what they are experiencing. This can make reaching out difficult, and it can make finding new friends especially challenging. Let me encourage you that one of the best places to invest the emotional and physical energy you do have is in connecting with people, even if you have not done much reaching out in the past. As I mentioned previously, you can join a grief group or find an activity to engage in such as volunteering. Go to church even if you have to sit in the back silently. Push yourself to speak to people. Doing this will help you move forward along your journey.

Work, school, or church acquaintances

There may be plenty of people who know you through work, school, church, or other means. When these people find out you have lost a loved one, they may struggle to know how to relate to you. Many of them will want to express sympathy but may worry about how you will receive what they have to say. Some may shrink from involving you in conversations or other activities for fear of adding to your discomfort.

It's OK to feel hurt when people don't respond to you as you wish they would, but don't stay parked there. Think through some responses in advance that you can have ready in these situations. For example, if someone expresses sympathy, you can simply say, "Thank you. It means a lot to hear that from you." If there's an activity or conversation you need or want to be included in but sense others' hesitation, you can say, "Yes, I'm grieving. But I need and want to be here. Count me in." If someone seems reluctant to bring up your loved one, you might wish to break the ice and say, "Thank you for just speaking to me. Since my loved one died, it's harder for me to take the initiative, and I just appreciate a moment to connect with you."

Remember that your emotions are likely to be more sensitive than usual. You may take offense at others' words or actions more easily than normal. That's understandable, but it's also something you will need to move past. Most of the time people don't wish to cause you pain. It's about their prickly personality or lack of understanding, not about you. Many times your best choice is to simply move on.

You also may need to consider carefully what responsibilities you can and cannot continue during the early period of your grief. Most work supervisors, for example, will understand that you will not have 100 percent to give for a while and may be willing to offer modified hours or responsibilities. Don't be afraid to have an open conversation with teachers, supervisors, or others about making adjustments if needed.

Prickly people

Some people seem to sprout spines that prick you whenever you get close. These prickly people can be especially challenging while you're grieving. Whether intended or not, their words or actions cause you pain, and your diminished resilience makes it harder than usual to deal with them.

Give yourself some grace here. As you regain strength while continuing along your journey through grief, you will become better able to handle these people in the future. But for now it's OK to do what you need to protect yourself. You don't have to lash out in anger or become prickly yourself. When possible, simply avoid those people who make you feel worse.

Sometimes you can't completely avoid interacting with these prickly people. If you must interact, imagine putting a boundary around your heart. For this hour or this day you are superficial and polite, but you keep your grief temporarily under cover and don't make your heart vulnerable to them. You intentionally keep your heart protected. Then when that hour or day is over, perhaps when you're alone or with a safe friend, you take the boundary down and allow your grief to bubble up again.

Signs You May Need Urgent Help

Part of not grieving alone is recognizing when you may need a more intense level of help. Remember, in your original design God did not want you to experience grief. You were not hard-wired for this. Yes, He has gifted you with what you need to get through this, but sometimes that includes getting some higher-level help. And sometimes that becomes an emergency.

Here are some warning signs that can alert you to the need for some urgent help.

- Your inability to sleep continues for a prolonged period.

- You are unable to do simple things such as eat, get dressed, or obtain necessary items at the store.

- You have continued thoughts of dying or harming yourself or have a plan to do so.

- The same emotion, thought, or issue keeps you stuck for a prolonged period.

- You continue to feel no emotions weeks or months after your loved one's death.

- You feel you are making no progress in your grief work even though you are putting in regular effort.

- You are unable to form thoughts and carry them through.

- Your physical health is deteriorating.

- You are unable to connect with others for even brief periods.

There's no magic checklist to tell you that you are grieving "correctly." Grief is hard, confusing, exhausting, and a whole lot of other things. But if you're not making progress, know that you don't have to be stuck alone. There is help available.

If you are feeling suicidal, get some help *now*. Call a crisis hotline in your community. Call a friend. Call the National Suicide Prevention Lifeline anytime day or night: 1-800-273-8255. Get to an emergency room. Call 911 if you can't think of anything else to do. You are not the first person to feel the way you do, and there are people who want to help.

Keep in mind that seeing your physician is an important part of getting help. Medical care will not make your grief go away, but there may be important physical steps you need to take. At times, medication may be an important part of your journey through the dark valley of grief.

You may need some help specifically with your grief work. Admitting you need that help is a measure of strength and wisdom. Ask your friends, pastor, or funeral director for a referral if needed. Look for a Christian counselor or therapist who has skills and training in helping people get through the challenges of grief. Because every human being dies, people everywhere can struggle with grief. You're not the first one who has needed help. It's OK to ask for that help when you need it.

Trying to go through grief alone is unwise and unnecessary. While others cannot grieve for you or take your pain away, God created you to need support in this journey. Your relationships with family, friends, and acquaintances will change as a result of your loved one's death; that's expected and can even lead to positive changes. You will also have opportunities to develop new relationships along the way.

Intentionally investing some of your precious energy in connecting with people is an important part of doing your grief work and walking forward through this dark valley. That's one of the most important choices you can make at this time. Don't grieve alone.

TWO STEPS FORWARD

1. Have certain relationships become more painful since your loved one's death? How can you let go of needing to make those relation-ships work?

2. Who are you connecting with on your journey through grief? What do you specifically desire from those individuals? How will you go about asking for their support?

CHAPTER 6
SO MUCH STUFF

'What we have once enjoyed deeply we can never lose,
for all that we love deeply becomes a part of us.
—HELEN KELLER

DEATH OFTEN INVOLVES so much "stuff." Perhaps that's the most telling and final indictment against our materialistic and complicated society. The saying is true: you can't take it with you. And everything we accumulate is left for our loved ones to deal with.

Anyone who has lost a loved one will know how difficult handling practical matters can become. You may feel a lot of internal pressure to deal with all the stuff quickly. You may even imagine that once you have addressed all the stuff around your loved one's death, your pain will somehow go away. Most of the time any pressure you feel to do these things quickly is self-imposed. Yes, you will need to go through and make decisions about your loved one's belongings. Financial and/or legal issues will need to be addressed. But with only infrequent exceptions most of these matters do not have a time limit on them.

If you're on the other end of the spectrum and feel paralyzed as you contemplate all the stuff there is to deal with, there is good news. This is an area where you can usually move slowly and simply take one step at a time as you feel able to do so.

Before we move ahead, a disclaimer is in order. I have no legal or financial expertise, and there are many circumstances in which you will benefit from obtaining the professional services of an accountant, tax professional, and/or lawyer. This chapter addresses financial and legal matters in a general way and provides some questions you may want to think about in handling all the stuff. Nothing in this chapter should be considered legal or financial advice.

Dealing with the stuff is a big part of simply doing the next thing. Again, you can almost always take your time with these matters. Just deal with one thing today, and the rest will still be there tomorrow.

Final Arrangements and Funeral Stuff

By the time you read this, you will likely have already made the initial decisions around your loved one's final arrangements, such as burial or cremation, funeral and/or memorial service, etc. If you are not your loved one's next of kin, you may not have been as involved in these initial decisions as you would have liked. Your loved one may have made some of these decisions in advance as well, which can significantly lessen the initial burden family members often feel. Or the circumstances around your loved one's death may have prevented the kind of final arrangements they and you would have desired. Yet regardless of the situation, these decisions can take an emotional toll.

Many funeral directors are caring professionals who work hard to provide important and sensitive services to family members at a critical time. But remember that they are businesspeople too. Family members can sometimes feel pressure to spend more money than they have for extras or upgrades as a way of demonstrating how much they loved the individual who has died. It's right and good to honor your loved one. But the amount of money spent on the casket, burial place, headstone, urn, crypt, newspaper notices, or any of the other funeral arrangements has nothing to do whatsoever with how much you loved—and still love—the person.

You may feel vulnerable and emotional about these initial decisions. But the choices you already made are now in the past; don't spend any of your energy wishing you had spent more or less. For any decisions yet to be made, keep in mind that money does not equal value. If your loved one was buried, for example, choosing and obtaining a headstone can usually be done at any time. Choose to ignore any pressure you feel to spend money as a demonstration of your love, and focus instead on what will be most meaningful and valuable to you in remembering your loved one.

Sometimes these initial decisions create significant controversy among family members. Do your best to not let any such conflict distract you from honoring your loved one. You're vulnerable. It's rare that every detail will have been exactly as you would have wished. This is one of those times when it's usually best to embrace and treasure anything good and meaningful from the experience of laying your loved one to rest and let the rest go.

Financial and Legal Stuff

Final arrangements cost more than most people realize. This significant financial stress can add even more pressure to your grief process at a time when you already feel overwhelmed. Take it one step at a time. Remember that your financial status says nothing about your love for your loved one or your value as a human being. Hold on to that truth, and let God speak to you deeply about that if you struggle in this area. He knows you're battling with this; talk to Him about it, and seek both His peace and His guidance.

You are likely to have to deal with many of the following items that have large or small financial implications:

- bank accounts
- credit cards
- Social Security
- life and/or health insurance
- medical bills
- investment, savings, or brokerage accounts
- safety deposit box

- mortgage and home insurance

- subscriptions (such as for magazines, entertainment services, cell phones, etc.)

- vehicle(s)

You may find it helpful to make a list of the items you will need to address. Your funeral director may have provided you with such a list; that can be a good starting point. Some of these items will be simple; others will be frustrating and take some time to tackle. Of all the things I had to deal with after my husband's death, one of the most emotionally difficult for me was canceling his cell phone. It meant I would never hear his voice on the phone anymore. You may find handling some of these matters triggers emotional waves of grief you were not expecting. That's normal. Pause if you must and let the emotional wave wash through you, and then do the next thing.

Be on the lookout for God's ways of blessing you in these practical matters. I believe He takes special joy in showing you moments of grace when you are in the midst of grief. That doesn't mean things will be easy or that you will not face financial pressure. But keep looking for little things to thank God for: finding the key to the safety deposit box, a credit card or other bill in your loved one's name that is now canceled, an unexpected way to decrease some cost you were facing, a kind banker or customer service individual helping you navigate a challenge. Not everything will be smooth and not everyone will be kind, but be grateful when God blesses you in one of these small ways.

Your loved one's death may be the first time you have had to deal with legal matters such as those facing you now. Dealing with executors, estates, wills, probate attorneys, and bankers may seem intimidating. Again, remember that most of the time there is no rush in handling these matters. If you feel especially overwhelmed, ask someone you trust, such as an adult child or close friend, to go with you to the necessary appointments. This may help you feel less vulnerable. That individual also can help you remember what was said and be a sounding board as you talk through decisions you need to make.

You'll find that certain documents will be routinely needed, and you will build up a collection of new important paperwork. You may wish to create a special location for keeping all the documents you are likely to collect, such as your loved one's death certificate, newspaper notices, medical records, autopsy report (if done), legal documents such as will or executor delineation, insurance settlements, beneficiary statements, financial account closings or settlements, etc.

The task of dealing with all this stuff can seem endless. Remember, just do the next thing. Unless something is unusually pressing, don't let yourself feel rushed. You get no medal for speed. Just do the next thing, and ask for help when you need it.

Personal Belongings and Other Stuff

Much of the grief work you are faced with can be wonderfully helped by the process of going through your loved one's belongings. These personal items can provide a treasure trove of memories and may trigger deep feelings, both positive and painful. These personal effects may help you discover additional ways to honor your loved one, work through your grief, and embrace what your loved one meant to you and will always mean to you.

You may have friends or family members who offer to take care of your loved one's things for you. If at all possible,

The task of dealing with all the stuff can seem endless. Don't let yourself feel rushed. Just do the next thing, and ask for help when you need it.

don't let them do so. While it may seem terribly difficult, do it yourself. Take it as slow as you need to, but don't deprive yourself of this priceless opportunity to do your grief work.

There may be a drawer, a box, a closet, or even a room of your loved one's things that just feels too difficult to tackle. You may think you'll be emotionally overwhelmed if you open certain doors. That's OK. Take it one small step at a time. Perhaps today you can move that box out of the closet and closer to your chair, or maybe you open the door to that room just a crack. In another day or two you take the lid off that box or open the door a little farther. A little later you can pull the first item out of that box or turn on the light in that room. Even though the emotional work will feel difficult, your grief process will be greatly helped by slowly but persistently dealing with your loved one's belongings yourself.

Don't place yourself on a timeline for getting rid of your loved one's belongings. Take it in stages, and embrace the memories and feelings that come along the way.

For me, the process of going through my husband's things was very slow, and there are still some of my husband's things I haven't finished dealing with. I addressed it in stages. First, I got rid of everything connected with his medical care; I wanted to try to remember him not as sick but as healthy as possible. Next, I donated his glasses to an organization that could repurpose them for people who couldn't afford glasses, and I gave his business suits to an organization helping those in need look professional when they applied for jobs. Further steps have been slower still. Many of his things are still around my home, and I feel in no rush to remove them.

Don't place yourself on a timeline for getting rid of your loved one's belongings, and don't let anyone else put you on a timeline either. Take it in stages, and embrace the memories and feelings that come along the way. You'll have a sense of when it's time to take another step. Don't keep a shrine, but you may not want to get rid of some items at all, and that's OK.

Some of your loved one's items may be digital—computer

files, social media profiles, contact lists, digital photos, email accounts, and much more. These can be some of the more tedious matters to deal with. Again, there are no medals for speed; just do the next thing.

You may find some of your loved one's personal effects provide special opportunities to create lasting ways to remember him or her. Over the first months and even years after your loved one's death you may wish to be creative with some of these means of remembrance. There's no limit to the possibilities of things you can create: a shadowbox of items from the funeral, a scrapbook filled with memories, a slideshow or video of your loved one's life or of the funeral, a quilt made from pieces of your loved one's favorite clothing, a collage of photos, etc. This is another reason not to give in to the pressure some people feel to get rid of their loved ones' things quickly.

As you go through the person's belongings, it's possible you will discover something about your loved one you never knew before, perhaps even something you wish you had never found out. The risk is worth it. Each human being, including your loved one, is a mixture of mistakes and triumphs, good characteristics and bad, failures and successes. Part of your grief work includes framing your loved one in your mind in a way that embraces all of who he or she was and is, even the parts you may initially wish you didn't know about. The emotions you encounter along with these discoveries may be unpredictable, but they're part of the journey.

Fights Over Stuff

Family fights over who gets what after a loved one's death can be emotionally traumatic. Your emotional wishes, financial needs, and sense of fairness can all be impacted. Very rarely is there a right or wrong when it comes to dividing the stuff.

This is not a new problem. Luke tells the story of how Jesus responded to someone wrestling with this: "Someone in the crowd said to him, 'Teacher, tell my brother to divide the inheritance with me.' Jesus replied, 'Man, who appointed me a judge or an arbiter between you?' Then he said to them, 'Watch out! Be on your guard against all kinds of greed; life does not consist in an abundance of possessions'" (Luke 12:13–15).

Jesus was not saying that fairness, justice, money, and inheritance do not matter. He was saying that they are not the most important things. As painful as it may be to remember right now, the money you have or don't have and who gets or doesn't get certain of your loved one's belongings are temporary matters. While they may seem huge to you right now, there are things that matter more.

No one can take away the memories you have of your loved one. Material possessions may have meaning and be connected to important memories, but your memories are not dependent on the stuff. And in the eternal scheme of things, material possessions are far down on the list of what matters most. Don't lose the memories you have, or the peace, comfort, and hope you have in Jesus, by fighting over stuff.

◆

The death of a loved one almost always means you will have to deal with stuff—final arrangements, the person's physical and digital belongings, financial and legal matters, and more. The pressure to deal with these tasks can seem overwhelming or paralyzing. Sometimes family conflict over the stuff can be traumatizing.

Keep the stuff in perspective. Almost always these matters can be addressed slowly, one thing at a time and only as you feel able. Look for the small blessings that present themselves as you work through these matters, and be grateful for them. Embrace the bittersweet memories that working through the stuff can bring up as well as the opportunities they give you to do your grief work. Finally, remember that all stuff is temporary. Your loved one's memory, the life that person lived, and the relationships you shared are more important than money or things. Hold on to that memory tighter than you hold on to any of the stuff.

TWO STEPS FORWARD

1. Some people find it helpful to list the stuff they need to attend to and do one thing each day. If you feel scattered, consider making such a list.

2. Determine that you will go through your loved one's things yourself if at all possible. Choose to give yourself that opportunity to grieve well.

CHAPTER 7
DEATH IS NOT NORMAL

The darker the night, the brighter the stars
The deeper the grief, the closer is God.
—APOLLON MAYKOV

HOWEVER LONG YOUR loved one lived, it was not long enough. Whether you lost a child before she even took her first breath or your loved one enjoyed a full life and lived to be one hundred years old, it's never enough. Even if your loved one died after prolonged suffering and you feel immense relief now, there's part of you that knows he didn't live long enough.

And you're right; however long it was, your loved one's life was too short. God did not create you or your loved one to live a few years or even many years on this earth and then die. He created humankind to live forever. He created each one of us for eternity. Death was never part of God's original intention for you or your loved one. No wonder death feels so strange. No wonder we rage against it.

In some sense death seems normal here, in the sense that every human being dies. In human terms everything in this world eventually dies: animals, plants, people, civilizations. To have a human being or even a beloved pet *not* die would truly seem even stranger than death. But in God's universe as a whole, death is not normal. When God creates things, His original plan is not for them to exist only for a short time. Angels don't die. Animals and growing things don't die in heaven, and they won't die in the new earth God has promised to re-create. People won't die in the new earth either (Rev. 21:4). Death is a horrible aberration in creation, an intruder, something we rightfully see as an enemy (1 Cor. 15:26).

When I got home from the hospital the Sunday morning my husband died, I sat down with a cup of coffee and my Bible. I opened it to 1 Corinthians 15, Paul's treatise on death and resurrection. In this chapter we're going to look at that passage as well as others. We'll examine what God has to say about this subject that affects us all so deeply, the thing that God never originally intended you to experience but that defines your life so completely right now.

The Bible has a lot to say about death. If you haven't already done so, grab your Bible or open the Bible app on your smartphone, and get ready to highlight some of the passages we will explore as they speak to your heart. In the emotional vulnerability of your grief journey this chapter may seem somewhat heavier than others. You may want to come back to it again in the future. But I encourage you to read it now anyway. If your mind struggles in grappling with some of the theological ideas, simply let the overall picture of how Jesus and the New Testament believers viewed death speak to your heart. There is much hope here.

How Jesus Viewed Death

Jesus has only one attitude about death. He's against it!

Repeatedly throughout the Gospels we read about how death couldn't exist in Jesus' presence. He shows up and sick people get well. People simply don't die when Jesus is around. And several times when Jesus arrives shortly after someone has died, the person lives again. No wonder the people wanted to make Him their earthly king; they could go into battle and no soldier would die, or at least they wouldn't stay dead very long if Jesus was there.

People came to realize this relatively early in Jesus' public ministry. If they could get a sick person to Jesus (or Jesus to them) before he or she died, the individual would be made well. And if they could get Jesus there quickly enough even after someone had died, the person could live again.

This is not making light of Jesus' miracle-working power or of death. Far from it. But it's important to pause and understand how completely opposed to death Jesus was—and is. Death was powerless in His presence. There was never anything good or acceptable about death in Jesus' view.

Perhaps this raises the question in your mind: "I prayed, and my loved one still died. Isn't Jesus with us now? Couldn't He have kept my loved one from dying?" We'll talk about that more in the next chapter, but for now, I'll say this: Jesus was and is against death 100 percent. And while He was physically here on earth, humankind got a taste of the kingdom of God (Mark 1:15). Humanity got to see a little of what things become like when sin is gone and God reigns in completeness. There is no such thing as death when things are as God wants them to be.

Jesus and mourning

While He was 100 percent against death, Jesus was very much on the side of those who mourned. He didn't say, "Quit your grieving; it's not pretty." His message was, "Blessed are those who mourn, for they shall be comforted" (Matt. 5:4, MEV). When He came across a widow whose only son had just died, "He had compassion on her and said to her, 'Do not weep'" (Luke 7:13, MEV). When He saw how upset Mary and Martha were after their brother, Lazarus, died, "Jesus wept" (John 11:35). Though on each occasion He knew He was about to raise the person (the widow's son and Lazarus) from the dead, Jesus identified deeply with the loved ones' grief. And He feels the weight of your grief with you right now.

More importantly, Jesus wasn't content to just weep with those who weep; He came to do something about it. He came to do away with death. "Since the children have flesh and blood, he too shared in their humanity so that by his death he might break the power of him who holds the power of death—that is, the devil—and free those who all their lives were held in slavery by their fear of death" (Heb. 2:14–15). In a broad sense we can explain Jesus' whole mission on earth as dedicated to doing away with the cause, the results, and the very existence of death.

Because He was committed to eliminating death, Jesus also saw what we struggle to fully believe. Jesus could say things like "Very truly I tell you, whoever obeys my word will never see death" (John 8:51). And to Martha He said, "I am the resurrection and the life. The one who believes in me will live, even though they die; and whoever lives by believing in me will never die. Do you believe this?" (John 11:25–26).

Never see death? Never die? We spiritualize those statements away too quickly. We know from Scripture as a whole and from our own experience that death as we know it, the decay of our physical bodies, happens still today. But in these passages Jesus said the essence of a believer, the real "you" who was/is your loved one, never dies. Jesus says to you as He said to Martha, "Do you believe this?"

Physical vs. spiritual death

These statements of Jesus, and Paul's treatise on death and resurrection in 1 Corinthians 15, challenge us to remember that physical and spiritual death are not one and the same. In fact, they could not be more different. Yes, the human condition has a 100 percent mortality rate in terms of our physical bodies returning to dust, but that's only the death we see with our physical eyes. Your loved one has not ceased to exist. At my husband's home-going service, I placed my hand on his casket and declared, "This is not my husband! This is his body, but he is not here." We grieve physical death, and rightly so. Jesus, Paul, and all the New Testament believers never say we must not grieve. But they do encourage us to remember that what we're grieving is not the end or even ultimately the most important kind of death.

As believers we pay intellectual assent to the resurrection and eternity, and theologians argue about what they call "the state of man in death." But I believe these statements of Jesus point us to a reality we dismiss too quickly because of our human time-bound perspective. God is sensitive to how we experience time; He created time, and He created us within it. We hurt over a loved one's death in part because we can only experience this moment in time. But God Himself exists outside of time. To Him, yesterday, today, and forever are all present at the same time. And just as you don't waste one ounce of energy worrying whether the sun will come up tomorrow, your loved one's forever future is more real and "present" to God than his physical decaying body. (If you are concerned about whether or not your loved one is "present with the Lord," we'll address that in the next chapter.)

I struggle to find the words to express this, and you probably struggle to wrap your mind around it, especially as you are grieving. Martha struggled too. As Jesus was talking to her about Lazarus and the comparative smallness of physical death, "Martha answered, 'I know he will rise again in the resurrection at the last day'" (John 11:24). And when Jesus responded by declaring "I am the resurrection and the life," all Martha could do was simply affirm, "Yes, Lord, I believe that You are the Christ, the Son of God, who is to come into the world" (John 11:25–27, MEV).

Perhaps that's all you can do right now too. And that's OK. Choosing to embrace this truth does not remove the pain of your loss. It does not remove the blackness of your dark valley of grief, but it does point to the temporariness of it. This truth assures you that your pain will come to an end just as assuredly as the reality that death—physical death included—will die.

We appropriately rage against death because part of us senses it's not "normal." But again, remember that your loved one has not ceased to exist. Jesus' statements that we will "never die" and "never see death" are too overwhelming, too radical to dismiss. Theologians can argue all they wish about "the state of man in death," but we can believe Jesus' statements even if we don't understand every detail about them. In this sense God's original intent in our creation, that humankind would live for eternity, has never been thwarted. Sin has created a huge detour, to be sure. The physical bodies that God intended to be ours forever are now only temporary, but in eternity they will be changed into bodies that will never die (1 Cor. 15:52–54). God's purposes have never changed; your loved one is safe with Him. And we can know this much from examining Jesus' view of death when He was here: Jesus is 100 percent against death, and because of Him death will have an end.

In the meantime imagine Jesus being next to you right now, as He was next to Mary and Martha. You can cry out, as they did, "If You had been here, my loved one would not have died!" And you can see Him weep with you, comfort you, hold you close. And even though it's beyond our complete understanding right now, know that He understands. How can He be so against death and still be that present with you right now in your grief? In some ways that's one of the paradoxes of the kingdom of God. It's fine to ask the questions. And while you're feeling undone and hoping for the answers, just affirm with Martha, "Jesus, I may not understand. But I believe that You are who You say You are and that You are in the process of making all things right."

How Early Believers Viewed Death

Jesus' resurrection was the most disruptive event ever to occur in human history. The entire order of things was upset. Humankind had been raging against death for thousands of years but was powerless to stem its tide even a little. The mortality rate was 100 percent. (Well, except for the special cases of Enoch and Elijah.)

Until Jesus.

Jesus had cracked the death code, found the cure, beat the odds, grabbed death—physical death as well as spiritual death—by the throat and made it bow. Nothing remotely like that had ever happened before. While some are reluctant to acknowledge it, there is considerable historical evidence for the physical death and resurrection of Jesus. And it wasn't because people didn't try to cover it up. The priests paid off the guards stationed around Jesus' tomb to change their testimony (Matt. 28:11–15). In the culture at large, affirming that Jesus was alive was more ludicrous than it would be to claim Elvis is alive today. (See Acts 4:2; 17:32; and 25:19.) For centuries those who dared to claim "Jesus is alive" and live accordingly put their own lives at risk (and in some places they still do).

And yet the early church grew. The eleven remaining disciples, the more than five hundred people who saw Jesus alive after His resurrection, and the growing number of those who believed He was alive were willing to die themselves because of that truth. Banishment, ridicule, lions, the stake, the rack, the sword, a cross—the very worst that human beings and demons could cook up couldn't dissuade believers from affirming that Jesus was alive and from living according to that belief. Could anything less than the truth have provided them that kind of unquenchable "blessed hope"? Jesus said, "Because I live, you also will live" (John 14:19), and the early Christians believed it.

Most of us Christians take it for granted that Jesus rose again. But imagine for a moment if that were not true. As Paul said, "And if Christ has not been raised, our preaching is useless and so is your faith.... And if Christ has not been raised, your faith is futile; you are still in your sins. Then those also who have fallen asleep in Christ are lost. If only for this life we have hope in Christ, we are of all people most to be pitied" (1 Cor. 15:14, 17–19). The reality of Jesus' resurrection changes everything, especially the reality surrounding physical death.

The early believers grieved over their loved ones who died, but they knew death would not have the last word. "The last enemy that will be destroyed is death" (1 Cor.

15:26, MEV). Death would die. "Then the saying that is written will come true: 'Death has been swallowed up in victory. Where, O death, is your victory? Where, O death, is your sting?'" (1 Cor. 15:54–55). Because of Jesus' resurrection, death is not the end. That changed the way the early believers saw death. They understood that sin in the world as a whole resulted in death—physical death and spiritual death. Jesus' death on the cross had dealt with it all—sin, death, evil, all of it. And now because of His resurrection, all that mess, including the death we mourn, was temporary. Painful beyond expression, yes, but temporary. And even the worst pain can be survived if it's temporary.

Present with the Lord

There's one more important understanding the early believers had about death: to be absent from the body is to be present with the Lord. "Therefore we are always confident and know that as long as we are at home in the body we are away from the Lord. For we live by faith, not by sight. We are confident, I say, and would prefer to be away from the body and at home with the Lord" (2 Cor. 5:6–8). This is not the time to engage in theological arguments trying to explain this in human terms, but it is a

> **Because of Jesus' resurrection, death is not the end. It's only temporary. And even the worst pain can be survived if it's temporary.**

precious truth. Paul was actually expressing his preference to go away and be with the Lord. Somehow, when this earthly body ends its existence, the real person is with the Lord.

You may struggle with that same desire—to die too and be "with the Lord." Paul says nothing about that desire being wrong in itself. But he hastens to add that voluntarily acting on that desire (causing one's own death) is not God's plan. (If your loved died as a result of suicide, we'll talk about that more in chapter 9.) Paul wrote, "For to me, to live is Christ and to die is gain. If I am to go on living in the body, this will mean fruitful labor for me. Yet what shall I choose? I do not know! I am torn between the two: I desire to depart and be with Christ, which is better by far; but it is more necessary for you that I remain in the body" (Phil. 1:21–24). Paul still had a job to do, and he embraced the mission God had for him as long as he was needed here on earth.

If you're breathing, God still has something for you to do here. You may not know what that is right now, and that's OK. The death of a loved one is one of those times when the meaning of life becomes very important to many people. When you're hurting so badly, it may seem preferable to forgo your purpose and just quit. But I can assure you, and others who have walked this journey before you can assure you too, that you won't always feel as you do right now. In wrestling with this myself, I've come to the decision that I'm OK with sticking around as long as God needs me here and not one moment longer. I believe that's the decision Paul came to, and I pray it's the decision you come to also. And it makes me even more determined to make what time I have left fully count for the kingdom of God. I pray you'll do the same.

Dear grieving friend, all you may be able to see right now is death. Death has robbed you of someone you loved, and your world appears to have ended. It may seem as though nothing could possibly be bigger than death. I understand as much as a fellow grieving human being can. Jesus understands completely. Your heart is broken into a million pieces, and you can't imagine it ever being any other way.

But while I have my arm around you and mix my tears with yours, I also bid you to look up! There is One who voluntarily entered death's territory for the purpose of destroying sin, fear, sickness, evil, bondage—and death. He deliberately and knowingly entered the open jaws of death, walked up to the keeper of the prison house of the grave, and wrested the keys from his hands. Then He walked out of His own grave, holding death's keys in His wounded hands and leading a train of freed captives behind Him as He declared the death of death.

Can't you see? The black and dark and universal enemy that has stolen your loved one is only a temporary and defeated foe. Hold on to that. This is the truth that allowed the early believers to grieve differently and to go cheerfully to their own physical deaths. And this is the truth that will allow you to ride the waves of hope that are offered to your soul even as the waves of grief wash over you. This pain is temporary, my dear friend. It's temporary! There's no bigger difference between believers and those who grieve without hope than this absolute and unshakable truth.

Our human view of death is understandable. Life on this earth has a 100 percent mortality rate. But Jesus entered death's territory for the purpose of destroying the cause, the results, and the very existence of death. His life on earth demonstrated that in His presence death has no power. And His resurrection declared forever the death of death. In the meantime Jesus views you who are grieving with overwhelming compassion and identifies deeply with your pain.

Early believers came to understand that because Jesus is alive, they too would live. In fact, in the ultimate sense they could never die. Earthly death and everything surrounding it, while painful, is temporary. And for the believer, when one's existence in this earthly body ends, one is then present with the Lord. While we may not fully understand what that means, we can receive comfort and hope in affirming that reality.

TWO STEPS FORWARD

1. Imagine yourself as Mary or Martha, mourning their brother's death. Imagine what Jesus would be saying to you right now. Write your thoughts in your journal.

2. What does "present with the Lord" mean to you? Based on what Scripture says about the concept, does that idea bring you any comfort?

CHAPTER 8
WHY, GOD?

Lord... if you had been here, my
brother would not have died.
—MARTHA, JOHN 11:21

WHILE YOUR EXPERIENCE of grief is unique, there are
more people around you who have experienced or are
experiencing grief than you probably realize. The leader
of a monthly prayer group I participate in asked me to
tell the group about the opportunity God has given me
to write this book, which I did for two or three minutes. Even I was surprised at the response. Many of the
group members came up to me later and told me about
their own loss—a child, a beloved older sister, a spouse, a
parent. And each one mentioned some variation of "I was
angry with God" or "This rattled my faith" or "I had a
hard time accepting that God would do this."

However your faith has been challenged in years past,
the death of a loved one can challenge your belief in, trust
in, and relationship with God in new ways. You may
be surprised at how deeply this affects you even if you

have had a close relationship with God in the past. Your questions may be unspoken or shouted aloud. You may be partially successful in covering them over with religious behaviors but only for a time. You won't wrestle with all these questions, but some part of you will almost certainly ask one or more of them:

- If God is good, why did He allow this to happen to my loved one? Why is He allowing me to suffer right now?

- If God is all-powerful, couldn't He have prevented my loved one from dying?

- Is God punishing me by taking my loved one from me?

- Did my loved one die as punishment for his sins?

- Does the fact that my grief is so excruciatingly difficult mean I'm not trusting God? Couldn't He make this journey easier? Why doesn't He do so?

- If God really cares, why is He letting all these bad things, including my loved one's death, happen?

- I prayed. Others prayed. Why didn't God answer our prayers?

- My loved one was not saved. Would a good God put him in hell?

Some part of you is almost certain to ask some variation of *why*.

There's good news and painful news in response to your questions. The good news is that there are answers. The painful news is that those answers probably won't be what you expect or want them to be. They probably won't intellectually satisfy your *why* in the way you may wish they would. The answers won't be the kind that would necessarily stand up in a courtroom or formulate a scientific proof.

But if you give God opportunity, if you choose to keep putting one foot in front of the other in your journey through this dark valley and invite Him to go with you, you can find the answers. Or perhaps more correctly, your questions can be satisfied.

Here are some ways to think about these questions and some suggestions for how to look for answers.

How to Ask Why

For as long as human beings have tried to survive in a sinful world, they have asked why. The problem of good and evil is perhaps the biggest of all questions, and when you lose a loved one, it becomes intensely personal. How can you reconcile a good God with the badness of what you're experiencing right now? Theologians and philosophers have wrestled with those questions for millennia, and we won't finish that discussion here. But as you go about asking those questions, there are some useful things to know and do that will help you move toward their resolution.

It's OK to ask questions.

Some people feel guilty for even asking *why* questions. Some of the people you discuss these issues with may give you the impression that "good" Christians don't ask such questions. They may offer "answers" that feel demeaning, superficial, insensitive, or meaningless. The first thing to know is that God's Word demonstrates that it's OK to ask these kinds of questions.

Here are just a few biblical examples of God's friends plying Him with *why* questions.

> So Moses returned to the LORD and said, "Lord, why have You brought trouble on this people? Why is it You have sent me? For since I came to Pharaoh to speak in Your name, he has done evil to this people; neither have You delivered Your people at all."
>
> —EXODUS 5:22–23, NKJV

> Have I sinned? What have I done to You, O watcher of men? Why have You set me as Your target, so that I am a burden to myself?
>
> —JOB 7:20, NKJV

> Why do You stand far off, O LORD? Why do You hide Yourself in times of trouble?
>
> —PSALM 10:1, MEV

> My God, My God, why have You forsaken Me? Why are You so far from helping Me, and from the words of My groaning? O My God, I cry in the daytime, but You do not hear; and in the night season, and am not silent.
>
> —PSALM 22:1–2, NKJV

O God, why have You cast us off forever? Why does
Your anger smoke against the sheep of Your pasture?
—Psalm 74:1, nkjv

O Lord, how long shall I cry, and You will not hear?
Even cry out to You, "Violence!" and You will not save.
—Habakkuk 1:2, nkjv

Martha said to Jesus, "Lord, if You had been here,
my brother would not have died."
—John 11:21, mev

God has no problem with you asking such questions.
Those who knew Him well—His very best friends—asked
those kinds of questions. The painful human emotions that
accompany grief, such as frustration, anger, desperation,
confusion, and fear, are real and God understands that.
Asking such disturbing questions is fine. In fact, wrestling
with such questions opens the possibility of an even
closer relationship with God in the future. It's possible
to shake your fist at God, demanding He do what you
want as though you're greater than He is; that's not what
we're talking about. But when you bring Him your deep
and troubling questions like a hurt child going to a loving
parent, you actually honor Him. So yes, ask.

Direct your questions to God.

In the biblical examples listed previously, notice that
these Bible heroes directed their questions to God. In fact,
He welcomes that: "Come now, and let us reason together,
says the Lord" (Isa. 1:18, mev). The Hebrew word translated

"reason" in this verse can also be translated "argue."[1] God invites us to come to Him with the tough questions. You won't hurt His ego or make Him mad.

In fact, God is the only reliable place to go for answers. Reading books like this one; talking with friends, family, and other believers; and searching your own mind for answers may all have their place. But there is an important sense in which one human (you) going to another human source for answers to the really big questions is like the blind leading the blind. At some point you need to go to the source. The only way in which this book or other believers are truly helpful in addressing these questions is when the Holy Spirit takes a thought or statement you read or hear and applies it to your own heart. He's the only One who knows the ultimate answers. And He's the only One who can speak those answers to the deepest places in your soul.

Get quiet so you can hear God's answers.

How do you hear God's answers? Often our thoughts and overwhelming emotions during a time of grief make hearing God's voice difficult. He doesn't usually shout over the clashing barrage of sound in your head. That's why it's important for you to find ways to get quiet. It's when your mind and heart have become relatively still that you are more likely to hear Him. You do that primarily by intentionally entering the presence of God and inviting Him to go with you into the deepest hurts and darkest places of your heart.

Find times when you can get alone with God. You

may be tired and emotional, and your mind won't have the same ability to focus as you normally do, but just be still. You may wish to begin by reading a few verses in the Psalms or listening to some worship music. You may cry or beg or scream. You may find journaling your prayers to God a helpful way of expressing your deep emotions. Let whatever emotions you have flow out to God, and then don't rush away. Stay there a little longer and choose to allow your heart to hear if He has something to say to you.

Sometimes you will feel nothing except an emotional release, a crashing of the emotional wave in your soul. Sometimes you may sense a simple presence, a quiet knowing from God that says, "I'm here." Sometimes you may sense something specific and clear that can become like an anchor you will be able to hold on to during your journey through the dark valley.

One friend told me about how lost she felt when her older sister died. Her sister had always been a rock of strength to her. She cried out to God, "Why did You take my rock away from me?" She clearly heard God's reply to her heart, "I am your rock!"

A wife was crying out to God in her grief after her husband's unexpected death. God spoke to her, "Be grateful." She replied, "How can I be grateful for his death?" God responded, "I'm not asking you to be grateful for his death; I'm asking you to be grateful for his life." And she felt an important change in the direction of her emotions from that point on.

Some weeks after my husband died, I was feeling his loss

deeply and wrestling with God about my pain. I heard Him clearly speak to my heart, "I trusted you to bring him home." That simple message to my soul encapsulated so much of the life Al and I had shared together, and it became a priceless reassurance to me of God's understanding, presence, and comfort, and that He had everything under control.

I remember a live event at which I heard evangelist Oral Roberts speak of how he and his wife wrestled deeply with God after their son Ronald's suicide. At one point God spoke to them, "I know something about this that you don't know." That became something they held on to in the ensuing years.

God will do the same for you. You may notice that God's simple message to these individuals during their grief was specific to them. You can hear His specific message just for you too. These examples hopefully will help you see how God's answers to your struggles and questions may not always satisfy your intellectual curiosity, but they will satisfy your soul. He will respond to you in a way that uniquely addresses what you need to hear. If you keep coming back into His presence, God Himself will become the answer to your questions.

Your job? Just keep coming back to Him. Find times, even if they're short, when you will intentionally enter God's presence. Do it over and over again. When you're there, let your emotions flow out and then get quiet. Direct your questions to Him. Stick around, and your questions can be satisfied.

Moving Toward Some Answers

For the remainder of this chapter I'm going to present a few ideas that have helped people move toward some resolution when it comes to asking, "Why, God?" Each of these ideas is itself worthy of deeper Bible study. But when you're feeling overwhelmed in the early periods of grief, what you need most is God's presence and comfort. This is only a brief overview of the topics addressed, but that may be all your brain can absorb right now anyway. Don't get too tied up in intellectual stuff. Let these truths speak to your heart.

The character of God

Nothing provides us greater security than truly understanding the character of God. The Bible as a whole is the story of how God originally intended things to be; how things got messed up; and all that He has done, is doing, and is about to do to make things right. Here are a few of the things we can be sure of about God's character.

God is full of love. His very nature is love always.

There are dozens of variations of this truth in Scripture.

> Give thanks to the LORD, for he is good. His love endures forever.
>
> —PSALM 136:1

> God is love.
>
> —1 JOHN 4:8

God never changes. He is always the same.

> Jesus Christ is the same yesterday and today and forever.
>
> —HEBREWS 13:8

God is never pleased when someone dies, either physically or spiritually.

> For I take no pleasure in the death of anyone, declares the Sovereign LORD. Repent and live!...Say to them, "As surely as I live, declares the Sovereign LORD, I take no pleasure in the death of the wicked, but rather that they turn from their ways and live. Turn! Turn from your evil ways! Why will you die, people of Israel?"
>
> —EZEKIEL 18:32; 33:11

God takes your loved one's death seriously. It's important to Him.

> Precious [noteworthy, important] in the sight of the LORD is the death of His saints.
>
> —PSALM 116:15, NKJV

God knows everything that we don't know.

> For as the heavens are higher than the earth, so are My ways higher than your ways, and My thoughts than your thoughts.
>
> —ISAIAH 55:9, MEV

God will wipe away all your tears.

> He will swallow up death forever. The Sovereign LORD will wipe away the tears from all faces.
>
> —ISAIAH 25:8

> He will wipe every tear from their eyes. There will
> be no more death or mourning or crying or pain,
> for the old order of things has passed away.
>
> —REVELATION 21:4

Marinate in these truths about who God is. Let them sink into your soul. Saturate your thoughts with these ideas. Sometimes when nothing makes sense intellectually, the only thing you have to hold on to is that you know who your God is. Your feelings may not be there, but you can choose to trust anyway.

These truths about who God is can be especially helpful if you are not sure of your loved one's salvation. Remember, God cannot act in a way that is inconsistent with His nature. He's not looking to keep your loved one out of heaven; He's looking for any possible way to save him or her. You almost certainly don't know what happened between your loved one and God in the final moments of the person's presence on earth. It only took a quick "Lord, save me!" for Jesus to rescue Peter from drowning (Matt. 14:29–31). With one simple outcry to Jesus, the thief on the cross was assured of his salvation (Luke 23:42–43).

Did your loved one call out to Jesus in the final milliseconds of his or her life? You and I don't know, but God does. Remember, He is not willing for anyone to perish. The witness of Scripture is that not every human being will be saved, but if there's any possible way for God to save your loved one, He will do so!

And what if your loved one is not there when God makes all things new? Some people feel they would never be able to enjoy eternity without their loved one. This is again where relying on the character of God is important. You and I can be assured that in eternity, when we are able to see everything and know everything as God does, when we can ask Him our remaining questions face to face, we will not want Him to have done anything differently. We will be able to affirm, "He has done all things well" (Mark 7:37, NKJV).

These next ideas address theological points where good, God-fearing Bible students sometimes disagree. I hope you find these ideas helpful. But please don't get bogged down here if you don't.

> **In eternity, when we are able to see and know everything as God does, when we can ask Him our remaining questions face to face, we will not want Him to have done anything differently.**

The nature of good and evil

We live in a war zone. Our entire sinful, messed-up world is a war zone. Taking the war between God's kingdom of light and Satan's kingdom of darkness into account is perhaps the only way we can make much sense out of much that is going on around us, including the reality of death. Death became a reality on earth the moment Satan convinced Adam and Eve to rebel against God, and we've been experiencing the fallout ever since.

Yes, Jesus definitively won the war against Satan, sin, and death through His life, death on the cross, and resurrection. The war has been won eternally. But we live in the in-between time, that period between the reality of victory (at the cross) and the final realization of that victory (when God makes all things new). In this in-between time we often get wounded in the crossfire between good and evil. Our loved ones often get wounded. It's not fair! But it is part of the answer to the *why* questions. Why doesn't God eliminate evil when it hurts His children so deeply? Part of the answer involves God's determined desire that human beings follow Him, not because they are forced to do so or out of fear but because they love Him and choose to follow Him. That's only a partial answer, and I realize no rational answer will fully satisfy your heart.

Sometimes we get wounded—and our loved ones get wounded—through our own actions, choices, and behaviors. Sometimes we are wounded through the actions, choices, and behavior of others. And sometimes humans get wounded just because we are still living in this sinful, messed-up world. The good news is that regardless of the immediate cause, we know the end of the story. We can experience real healing, joy, and life here and now, but we don't experience all of that as fully as God originally created us to—at least not yet. Part of our redemption awaits eternity.

Paul wrote, "For we know that the whole creation groans and labors with birth pangs together until now. Not only that, but we also who have the firstfruits of the Spirit, even we ourselves groan within ourselves, eagerly waiting for the adoption, the redemption of our body" (Rom. 8:22–23, NKJV).

There is something we are still waiting for. That something yet to come will be more glorious, more wonderful, and more worth it than anything we can imagine.

Until then we can hold on to the rest of the story, which we know. Spoiler alert: Jesus wins!

Unanswered prayer

Sometimes the death of a loved one can be especially painful for Christians who firmly believe God answers prayers and performs miracles today. Why didn't God protect or heal your loved one? Was it because of your lack of faith? Your loved one's lack of faith? Your sin? Your loved one's sin? Should you have prayed harder? Could you have somehow drummed up more faith? Why didn't God answer your prayers and honor your faith?

Personally, I believe God performs miracles today. I've seen and experienced them myself. I've watched God perform miracles in answer to my prayers. I've also seen people not healed and people die, including my husband, even when prayed for in faith. I don't pretend to have answers that will explain everything, but I have learned much about what faith and prayer are all about.

God is not some heavenly vending machine who gives us what we want if we only find the right prayer formula. Faith is not some heavenly currency that allows us to get a certain outcome in exchange for a given quantity of faith. The kingdom of God being here on earth now does not mean everything always happens in the way we wish. Such a view actually cheapens faith and prayer, and it turns our relationship with God into a transaction. God's too big for that.

God describes Himself as our Father. If you are a parent, you understand that your view of reality, life, and your children's well-being is much bigger than theirs. So is God's view of reality and our well-being. He suffers with us when we suffer. Pain and death are not good things. God doesn't enjoy your pain and isn't trying to teach you a lesson by taking your loved one from you. Not at all! But there are things He knows that we don't know.

There's also the issue of time. Your pain right now is real, and if you could see Jesus with your physical eyes, I believe you would see Him right next to you, sharing your tears and holding you close. But He also sees the future. He sees the time when He will wipe away all your tears, and He knows it will be enough. He knows you will be completely satisfied. As a loving parent sympathizes with a toddler's angst over not getting an ice cream or skinning her knee, so God truly sympathizes with you. But He also knows, like you as a parent do, that tomorrow truly will be wonderful. That's how we can have hope even while we wrestle with the *why* questions.

Just Ask

During your journey through the valley of grief, worship may look different from how it looks at other times in your life. Whether you're spending time with God alone or in corporate settings, worship may look a lot like honesty. Remember that you honor God—you worship

Him—when you bring the rawness of your pain and your tough *why* questions to Him.

Let me close this chapter by simply encouraging you to keep on asking. Direct your questions to God. Go into His presence often. If you're feeling emotional, let those emotions flow out in His presence. And then stick around a little longer. Allow your soul to become quiet and listen for what He may have to say to you. While the questions will not all be answered in a way that satisfies your intellect, He will answer them in a way that can bring peace to your soul. He will become the answer.

The death of a loved one triggers *why* questions for most believers. The Bible demonstrates that asking such questions of God is appropriate and can lead to an even deeper relationship with Him going forward. Get all the input from others that you need, but remember to go to Him as the source for your answers.

Returning again and again to what you know about the character of God will help some as you wrestle with your questions. We presently live in a war zone between the kingdom of God and the kingdom of darkness, and you and your loved ones often get wounded in the crossfire. But you can know for certain that the day is coming when death will end and God will make all things right forever. And we will all be able to say, "He has done all things well."

TWO STEPS FORWARD

1. What are some of your *why* questions? Who are you asking about them? Are you asking God?

2. Set aside perhaps fifteen minutes and write a few emotional-type questions in your journal as a prayer to God. Then ask Him to speak to you as you sit quietly to hear from Him.

CHAPTER 9

COMPLICATIONS OF GRIEF

The course of true love never did run smooth.
—WILLIAM SHAKESPEARE, *A MIDSUMMER NIGHT'S DREAM*

THERE IS NO "pain meter" that can quantify your grief. How others perceive your loss may not correlate very well with the degree of impact your loved one's death has had on you. Every circumstance is unique. And yet there are circumstances surrounding some deaths that often prolong or complicate the journey through the dark valley of grief.

If your loved one was ill for some time or was quite elderly, you may have experienced anticipatory grief. I experienced that as a result of my husband's long illness. The questions, the sense of loss, the disorientation and pain are still there. But in such cases it's possible you may have worked through some aspects of your feelings even before your loved one's death. Your journey through grief will still be difficult, but it may not be quite as long as it can be for someone whose loved one dies without warning.

When your loved one dies as a result of murder,

suicide, natural disaster, accident, medical error, war, or other trauma, you may face extra challenges in your journey. Some experts say some of these circumstances may add an extra year or more to your journey through grief. Your life also may have been complicated in other ways around the time your loved one died, such as with other relationship or financial challenges, work issues, or your own health concerns. Stillbirth, miscarriage, and neonatal death present some unique challenges in the grieving process also.

You may find yourself ruminating over some of these dreadful details as much or more than the actual death of your loved one. No one can tell you how long this journey can, will, or "should" take. If some of these extra circumstances surround the person's death, know that others have made it through this journey even with such extra trauma, and you can too. Whether or not the specific circumstances have been mentioned here, if additional trauma shrouded your loved one's death, addressing the following issues may prove especially useful for you.

Recognizing True and False Guilt

Almost everyone going through grief feels some regret. Should you have said or done something different? If you had "stayed longer," might your loved one not have died? Did you miss warning signs indicating your loved one was in danger? Could you have done anything more or different to prevent the person's death? Did you do enough to let your loved one know how much he or she meant to you before it was too late? A million similar questions may flood your mind. Feelings of regret are perhaps universal. But if not dealt with, those regrets can develop into a serious burden of guilt.

It's important to understand that your feelings in this area do not necessarily correlate with reality. Your feelings are real, certainly. But just because you feel guilty about something does not mean you necessarily could or should have done anything differently. Sometimes what you're feeling is false guilt—an emotional sense of responsibility when you were/are not responsible at all. That feeling can be immobilizing, and if left unaddressed, it can become destructive.

Just because you feel guilty about something does not mean you necessarily could or should have done anything differently.

It's also true that you are a sinful human being. You may know of pain you caused your loved one and now look back with a heavy heart and a load of true guilt. You may find yourself ruminating about less-than-loving things you said or did, or things you failed to do. While it's likely that most of the guilt you feel is false, it is possible you may feel guilty about harm to your loved one that you truly caused or could have prevented.

How do you go about handling all this guilt? It helps to consider the significant portion of your emotional burden that may be false guilt. It was not your responsibility to make your loved one comply with medical recommendations or stop drinking or stay away from certain friends. Embrace the reality that God gives each human being free will, and you are not ultimately responsible for your loved one's thoughts, choices, or behavior. Sometimes there's truly no one to blame. Tragedy strikes in this sinful, messed-up world, causing us to yearn even more for eternity.

But in practical terms, attributing some of your feelings to "false guilt" is rather intellectual. If you feel stuck here, it may indicate you could benefit from professional help from a pastor or Christian counselor. Thinking through your guilty feelings may help, but it may not be enough to address your entire emotional burden. In the end the only effective way to deal with guilt is to give it to Jesus. You may not even be able to fully sort out where your false guilt ends and true guilt begins. We all have done things that caused others pain or that failed to prevent it. Only Jesus can remove that kind of guilt. His shoulders are the only ones big enough to carry it.

So if you feel burdened with guilt, true or false, hand it over to Jesus. Do this by claiming His promise that "if we confess our sins, He is faithful and just to forgive us our sins and cleanse us from all unrighteousness" (1 John 1:9, MEV). Enter into His presence and turn your regrets, failings, weakness, less-than-loving words and behavior, and everything else over to Him. If you've never really done that before, this is a great time to make things right with God. If you have done this in the past, your journey through grief will only be helped by doing this again.

Some may say, "I've asked God to forgive me, but I still feel guilty." First, separate guilt from regrets. Although I loved my husband well, I did so far from perfectly. Looking back, there are clearly things I wish I had done differently. It will almost certainly be the same for you. But as far as the guilt is concerned, step off that merry-go-round. If God says you're forgiven, who are you to disagree with Him? Choose to accept His forgiveness, repeatedly if necessary, and then choose to move on. Your feelings will eventually catch up.

Finding Freedom Through Forgiveness

Your mind may be searching for someone to blame for your loved one's death. In the last chapter we talked about wrestling with God and asking Him the *why* questions. Besides God, there may be people you hold responsible, perhaps rightfully so. You may feel angry at your loved one who didn't stop smoking or drinking, or follow medical advice, or took her own life. Perhaps the doctor missed the diagnosis until it was too late, or the medical personnel caring for your loved one messed up. Maybe the police didn't catch the bad guy when they had the chance, or the system let the offender out of jail so he or she was free to kill your loved one. The company, the government, or some other entity put profits ahead of safety, or they didn't do enough to keep your loved one from obtaining the drugs or gun he used to kill himself. You think that if someone—anyone—had cared a little more at any point along the way, you wouldn't be experiencing this pain now.

Feeling bitterness and anger at those partially or solely responsible for your loved one's death is only human, even if the responsible party is your loved one himself. It's natural to think, "It's not fair! How could he do this?" But we all are flawed. As the saying goes, to err is human. The health care system, the justice system, the government, the church, the military—they're all made up of flawed human beings who make mistakes, sometimes out of uncaring or evil hearts and sometimes despite the best of intentions.

And to top it off, there is the matter of evil itself. Tragically there are people in our world who act evil out in destructive and lethal ways. Sometimes first responders or military personnel are killed doing their best to push back evil and bring peace. Sometimes evil people's actions directly cause innocent deaths, perhaps including that of your loved one. Sometimes human institutions themselves act in evil ways. Evil is real.

When people or institutions are not acting in accordance with laws and decency, it's right to hold them accountable using any lawful means available, flawed though those means may be. Advocacy is appropriate. Many people who have lost a loved one through someone else's actions have used their pain to fuel changes in systems that make things better for others. If specific illegal acts caused your loved one's death, the ones doing those acts should be held accountable in the courts.

But that still doesn't address the anger in your own

heart. Holding on to bitterness will kill you, even if it does so slowly. Dealing with the matter of forgiveness is not primarily for the benefit of others; it's primarily to help you. It's the only way to be set free from the darkness enveloping your soul. There are many misunderstandings about what forgiveness is and isn't, and it's important to get this right. It's been said that refusing to forgive is like drinking poison and expecting the other person to die. That's not what God wants for you.

Forgiveness does *not* say everything is OK. It's not OK! That's the reason forgiveness is the only way to move forward. Forgiveness does not excuse the person or persons responsible for your loved one's death. Forgiveness means you give up your right to exact revenge on the one causing you pain and allow God (and appropriate authorities) to determine what kind of pain, if any, those responsible will experience. As Paul said, "Beloved, do not avenge yourselves, but rather give place to God's wrath, for it is written: 'Vengeance is Mine. I will repay,' says the Lord" (Rom. 12:19, NKJV). Forgiveness means you let the person who wronged you "off the hook" in your mind. You let them go.

Forgiveness is a step toward freedom.

You know God asks you to forgive those who hurt you; there are many Scripture passages to verify that. But that doesn't mean it's easy. Forgiveness isn't a feeling; it is something you have to choose. It's a decision, one you will perhaps have to make repeatedly. You can forgive even if the one you need to forgive refuses to acknowledge his role in your loved one's death or in your pain, or is even still alive. You may have to forgive your loved one himself. But forgiveness is a step toward freedom.

Please keep in mind that forgiveness does not eliminate all consequences of bad behavior. If a crime was committed, legal consequences may follow. If the persons involved continue their bad behavior, you may not be able to continue a relationship with them. In some cases our human systems cannot provide appropriate consequences, and bad behavior continues anyway. Even if that happens, through forgiveness *you* can still be free.

So how do you do that? How do you forgive when it feels impossible?

You do so in the same way you're going through this grief journey: one step at a time. You acknowledge your enormous pain and then decide to move toward forgiveness. This may be because the burden is too heavy to continue to carry or perhaps because your heart hears from God that forgiveness is the next step you need to take. Whatever the case, you move forward by acknowledging the poison of continuing to hold on to bitterness. And then you lay all that pain and anger down at Jesus' feet.

If you need to forgive someone, consider praying something like this:

> *Jesus, I'm hurting so bad right now. I'm so bitter and angry at* [whoever harmed you or your loved one]. *It's not fair! It's not right! I don't*

feel like forgiving them at all. But continuing to hold on to this poison in my soul will destroy me. And You have also asked me to forgive. I'm not sure I know how to do that, but I choose to let this go. I choose to allow You to decide what kind of pain they will get for their bad behavior. I choose to not allow their sin to continue to wound me more. I turn this over to You. I accept Your forgiveness where I need it, and I ask for Your grace to forgive. Amen.

While most of the medical care my husband received was exemplary, several bad events during the final twenty-four hours of his life in the intensive care unit left me very hurt and angry. I will never know for sure whether how he was cared for during that time hastened his death. For weeks afterward I would occasionally lie awake at night overwhelmed with tears and bitterness. I talked with the appropriate people in authority about my concerns. I wrote carefully worded letters. I even consulted with a few attorneys. But once these avenues were exhausted, the time came when I had to let it go. For my own mental, physical, and spiritual well-being I had to forgive. I had to let God, the only One who knew the whole truth, handle the consequences.

Hard though it may be, I wish for you the freedom of forgiveness.

Grieving the Additional Losses

The loss of your loved one's presence is almost always just one of many losses you are experiencing. Each of those losses needs to be grieved in turn.

You may have experienced the death of other loved ones in the past and have never fully explored your feelings and done the appropriate grief work to integrate their memory into the rest of your life. The death of the loved one you are grieving now may open wounds from previous loved ones' deaths, forcing you to realize that certain hurts have gone unhealed. See your current journey through the dark valley of grief as an opportunity to finish grief work that may be left over from previous loved ones' deaths. Multiple losses piled on you close together may mean your grief journey will take longer, and that's OK.

It's important to take the time to notice and grieve the other losses surrounding your loved one's death. Some of these losses will need only a brief acknowledgment; others may be as or more significant than the physical death of your loved one. You may have lost the intimacy of a marriage partner, the focus of caring for a loved one who was ill, the confidence that comes from a parent or sibling supporting your dreams, the financial support your loved one provided, or a certain social position because of your relationship with your loved one. Or perhaps you are having to leave the home you shared with your loved one. Or maybe because of the transitions in your life you will be unable to continue to enjoy the companionship of a beloved pet. Each one of these losses demands to be honored and grieved. For some of them you will want to do focused work to remember and grieve what was and then carry that memory forward with you in some meaningful way.

Challenges to the Grieving Process

No book can address every possible complication surrounding grief, but hopefully you will find some helpful comments here. These are some of the circumstances that can make your journey through the dark valley of grief even more challenging.

No body

"Missing" or "presumed dead" are some of the most painful words any family member can hear. I'm not sure there's ever any such thing as closure, but without your loved one's body, your grief has no place to land. You have mountains of unanswered questions. Among them are: How long do I keep hoping for a different outcome? Will I ever know what happened? Is my loved one still out there somewhere? The unanswered questions may leave you frustrated and angry with the authorities responsible for investigating the circumstances.

As with those who have laid their loved one to rest, you will almost certainly carry the questions and loss more acutely and much longer than others around you. Family, friends, and others may come around you initially, but then go about their lives while you're left with the questions and the pain. You're left in limbo, a no-man's-land.

You may not even be sure if this is a valley of grief you're trapped in or something else.

Even without a body to lay to rest, you can still create a memorial, a way to remember your loved one. Whether you create a scrapbook, plant a tree, or make something from items that belonged to your loved one, doing something to remember and honor your relationship with your loved one can be helpful. And don't forget to stay connected with others during your journey. Ask about military family's groups, victim's groups, survivor's groups, or other appropriate groups in your area or online where you can connect with others who are facing similar circumstances.

Grieving with children

Children grieve too, even though their grief is likely to look different from yours. If you are the parent or caretaker of a child who lost a parent, sibling, or other person close to them, be alert to the ways your child is processing his or her grief. Many children will grieve intermittently; they will feel and express strong emotions one moment, and then take a break with laughter and play the next. Allow your child to be a child. It's normal for your child's school grades, appetite, and energy level to change. Allow your child the same grace you want others to allow you during the grieving process. It can be helpful to clarify family roles, especially when a parent has died. For example, don't give the message verbally or nonverbally that a male child must now be "the man of the house."

Children, especially young children, usually see the world as revolving around them. That means they may have unique beliefs about your loved one's death that you need to watch for and lovingly correct. A young child may believe his own harsh words, angry thoughts, or disobedience caused his parent's or sibling's death, or that your loved one "left" because she was angry with the child. Children may worry that you will "leave" too or that they will die themselves. Lovingly and persistently talk about these beliefs in an age-appropriate way, and correct wrong thinking when necessary. Look for opportunities to talk about your loved one in ways meaningful to the child. Help the child remember your loved one in healthy ways. Be authentic. Model for your child that it's OK to cry, be sad, and talk about your loved one.

If your child's behavior becomes erratic or out of character, a skilled professional may be helpful. Don't feel as though you are a failure as a parent if your child needs this kind of assistance. Helping your child through grief can feel overwhelming as you are walking your own journey through the dark valley. Your child needs you, but be sure to seek and accept help from others and from God along the way.

Miscarriage, stillbirth, or neonatal death

Mothers and fathers who were looking forward to welcoming a new life into their family, only to have that life end before or as soon as it began, face a special kind of grief. There's something uniquely tragic when the beginning of life and the end of life are juxtaposed so closely. In my medical work I've talked with parents who struggle with enormous guilt at such times; almost always that's false guilt. You may feel like a horrible failure, ashamed that you were unable to bring a healthy child into the world. You may feel your body has betrayed you. Sometimes you may feel angry at medical personnel involved in your care.

Your family and friends may or may not have known you were expecting a baby. Regardless, you feel this loss much more than those around you. That's OK. No future child can replace the one you lost; that baby will forever be in your heart. Our culture often doesn't provide the same rituals to honor infants, especially if you lost your baby early in pregnancy, as it does for other people who died, and that's unfortunate.

You may find it helpful to do something yourself to remember and honor your baby. How important this is to you will partially depend on how attached you felt to your baby and at what stage in pregnancy your child was lost. But if you are feeling grief, it's healthy and right to do something to honor your child. Plant a tree, create a scrapbook, or make a memory box of items with which to remember your child. You may also find encouragement and support by connecting with an organization such as Compassionate Friends or one of the many other support groups for parents who have lost a child.

And remember that God holds every life carefully in His hands. He grieves with you, even if other human beings do not. Are those lives lost in miscarriage or stillbirth "present with the Lord"? I have no biblical proof text to offer, but I believe the answer is yes. You have a precious and unique reason to look forward to heaven.

Death by suicide

Suicide carries a heavy stigma in our culture. Suicide rates have increased notably, up 30 percent or more in over half of US states since 1999.[1] If this is how your loved one died, the *why* questions you're facing are especially painful. Appreciating something of the pain that led your loved one to act in this way will not prevent your own tangled feelings. You may mentally blame the person who committed suicide, or others, for your pain now. You may deeply wrestle with shame, self-doubt, and concern about your loved one's eternity. Your regrets may feel like insurmountable mountains.

Your loved one's suicide was not about you. Please hear that. There's not one human being who has not failed his or her family in some way, including you. But your loved one died because he was in pain, not because of any failure on your part. Could you have prevented the person's death? Probably not. But even if you could have, your loved one's death was not about you. If you are wrestling with guilt about this, read the earlier sections in this chapter about guilt and forgiveness. Lay everything surrounding your loved one's death on Jesus; this burden is too big for you to carry on your own. His shoulders are the only ones big enough to handle the load. Each time you feel the heaviness threatening to overwhelm you, place it on Him again.

Is suicide the unpardonable sin? Absolutely not. Is it a sin? In one sense yes; God does not intend for human beings to take their own lives. But in a larger sense God knows what we don't know, including your loved one's pain. How much did your loved one truly know about the life God has available? What circumstances may have clouded her ability to hear and respond to God? And what may have happened in the last milliseconds of her life on this earth? Did she cry out to God in those moments?

Remember, God is not willing that any human being should perish. He wants your loved one with Him in heaven, and whether he or she committed suicide is not the primary factor that will decide where that person spends eternity. God understands all the many elements of your loved one's painful life. He loves each of us, including your loved one, infinitely more than we can imagine. You and I can be grateful that He knows everything and that He is in charge. You can safely trust Him with your loved one's destiny.

The death of a loved one is complicated, and some circumstances add even more complications to your journey through grief. If your loved one died as a result of trauma, homicide, suicide, accident, negligence, or miscarriage or stillbirth, your grief is likely to carry extra challenges.

Regrets are almost universal among those who are grieving, and that commonly involves guilt. It's helpful to separate true guilt from false guilt—feeling responsible for things beyond your control. But the best way to handle all guilt, especially true guilt, is to give it to Jesus.

Forgiving those who may have been instrumental in your loved one's death may be one of your biggest challenges. You do that by choosing to let God determine what consequences the person(s) involved will receive. It's the only way to eliminate the darkness from your soul, and it will set you free.

TWO STEPS FORWARD

1. Are you holding on to bitterness in your soul? Is there someone you need to forgive? Ask God to help you take the next step toward forgiveness.

2. Take time to write in your journal about the multiple losses you suffered as a result of your loved one's death. Do you need to grieve some of these additional losses?

CHAPTER 10
AMBUSHES OF GRIEF

The holiest of holidays are those
Kept by ourselves in silence and apart;
The secret anniversaries of the heart.
—HENRY WADSWORTH LONGFELLOW, "HOLIDAYS"

AN ITEM IN the grocery store. An unexpected fragrance. The sight of someone with a certain body shape or hairstyle. A date on the calendar. A song on the radio. A line in a book or phrase in a sermon. Ambushes of grief can catch you at the most uncomfortable times. You may anticipate some of the triggers that set off an ambush while many others may surprise you.

As you continue to walk through the dark valley of grief, you will begin to find a new normal. Your life will begin to follow a new routine. Things will never be as they were when your loved one was alive, but your disorientation will decrease. Through your grief work and your trust in God, one day follows another and life begins to feel a little less overwhelming. You don't quite feel like you're drowning anymore, and you can take a breath again.

And then an ambush hits. An area of your pain you thought was dealt with will suddenly feel nearly as fresh as it was the first day. The anger, sadness, fear, confusion, hopelessness, etc. will wash over you, making you wonder if you've made any progress at all.

Yes, friend, you have made progress. Ambushes of grief are normal, and they don't mean you have been marching in place. Everyone who goes through grief experiences moments when thoughts and feelings about their loved one seem to take over their mind and body without warning. It's simply one more demonstration of how important your loved one was to you and of how large a place they occupied, and still occupy, in your mind and heart. Over time the ambushes of grief are likely to become less intense and perhaps less frequent, but they are likely to be part of your experience for a very long time.

Being aware of how ambushes of grief work can help you be better prepared when they strike and move through them more effectively.

Triggers

Countless sensory stimuli are connected with memories of your loved one. That's part of what made your life together as rich and complicated as it was. The circuits in your brain are physically laid down to connect certain sights, sounds, smells, touches, times, etc. with thoughts of your loved one. Think of those circuits in your mind as a highway where all the things you shared with your loved one—the memories, moments, objects, experiences, places, and more—all flow together.

Triggers can function like on-ramps to that highway in your mind. Sometimes the smallest thing can enter that on-ramp, and you're suddenly caught up in the speeding traffic of emotions. A torrent of thoughts and feelings associated with your loved one and their loss washes over you.

Some of those triggers you may identify relatively easily. You may smell a fragrance your spouse wore, hear a song your child used to sing, or drive past the hospital where your loved one received care. You may see a child the same age your child was when she died or would be now, or you catch sight of a couple enjoying an activity you used to enjoy with your spouse. You may come across an item of your loved one's that you had forgotten. At those moments you may find yourself tearing up or feeling irritable or overwhelmed in an instant.

Other triggers may be initially less obvious. You may experience something you would normally have shared with your loved one, such as a beautiful sunrise or a meaningful scripture. You hear or read something that in some way reminds you that your loved one is no longer physically with you. You may face a decision or a life challenge that you would have normally sought your loved one's help with, or you may simply feel tired or concerned. Something about that moment has triggered the memories and loss associated with your loved one, and the feelings wash over you.

Whatever the trigger, an ambush of grief is not

he llChristian's Journey Through Grief

something you can necessarily prevent. Once you determine what the triggers are, some part of you may wish to avoid those situations in order to not feel the waves of pain again, but doing so is often neither healthy nor completely possible. Sure, there may be certain things you avoid or don't enjoy any longer because of how they remind you of your loved one. But ambushes will still come. And they can become a useful part of continuing your grief work and walking further through this dark valley and toward the other side.

Dealing with ambushes of grief

When you find yourself ambushed by grief and speeding down that highway of thoughts and feelings in your mind, there are some things you can do to make it through the moment more effectively. Remember that feelings come in waves. The tears, confusion, anger, angst, or whatever emotions are flooding your mind will rise to a peak, and then they will lessen in intensity. When possible, pause and let the wave wash over you. Think of it as a reminder of how important your loved one was in your life.

The ambush may also alert you to some area of your grief work that still needs to be addressed, especially when the ambush feels overwhelming. After a difficult ambush of grief you may want to journal about it, and ask yourself and God what this may mean for your journey. Perhaps you need to spend some time with God addressing areas of guilt or forgiveness. Perhaps there are some additional steps you need to take to honor and remember your loved one. Perhaps there are some memories or feelings you need to explore further.

You may also find it helpful to plan in advance some things you will do when you feel an ambush of grief wash over you. Perhaps there is a friend or family member you will reach out to for support. You may choose to pause and speak to your loved one as though he or she was there, for your own benefit. Sometimes I will simply pause, look at my husband's picture, and say, "I miss you, honey!" If you're with people, you may choose to excuse yourself for a few moments, get alone, and cry briefly. I encourage you to include reaching out to God at those moments. Send up a prayer; "Jesus, this is hard. I need You right now!"

Ambushes of grief are an expected part of the journey. Choose to embrace them as valuable.

Over time the ambushes of grief may actually become precious to you. While they are likely to become less disruptive over time, their occurrence will continue to remind you of your loved one. It's one more way of keeping your loved one's memory alive in your heart. And that's a good thing. Ambushes of grief are an expected part of the journey. Choose to embrace them as valuable.

Dealing With Special Dates

Certain dates may be especially challenging emotionally and may trigger intense ambushes of grief. It's common for these dates to include birthdays (your loved one's, yours, or another family member's), anniversaries of your loved one's death, anniversaries of your marriage, or other important moments you shared. Times when your family members gather to celebrate a holiday or family event can remind you of your loss. Holidays of any kind can be difficult and intense.

The holiday season from Thanksgiving through New Year's is especially difficult for many who are grieving. You likely shared many holidays with your loved one and have memories from those times. Families often gather during this season, and a gathering without your loved one may seem terribly painful. The "first Christmas without..." is often dreaded. Many of your usual holiday traditions may seem too painful to engage in.

Many people experience holiday blues, and your grief may add more negative feelings to an already challenging time. The holidays frequently bring high expectations. Cultural messages often portray families gathering together around the holidays. The music, decorations, events, and expected gift-giving can add to the sensory overload, painful memories, and even depression. Some of those going through grief wish the calendar would magically skip from late November into early January.

Here are some suggestions for how you can make it through these special dates with less pain and more meaning even while walking through grief.

Care for your physical health.

Your emotions are much more volatile and harder to control when your physical body is not doing well. Especially during the first year or two after your loss, as special holidays or anniversaries come, you may need to return to some of the important ways you took care of yourself physically in the initial weeks after your loved one's death. That means remembering DEER: drink, eat, exercise, and rest.

Excessive and less-than-healthy food and drink, including alcohol, are often easily available at holiday events or family gatherings. While you may be tempted to indulge as a way to lessen your emotional turmoil, doing so will only add regret to your ambushes of grief. Choosing healthier options and smaller portions will help your brain manage your emotions more effectively.

If you're feeling upset, taking a nap or a walk may be a healthy option for both your body and mind. If you find yourself struggling with sleep during some of these periods, go back to the elements you found most helpful in dealing with sleep loss early on. (See chapter 3.) Make intentional choices about what to focus on as you prepare for sleep. Keep your sleep schedule as regular as reasonably possible.

Choose what to say yes to.

You don't have to attend every family gathering or holiday event. You don't have to continue every holiday tradition you and your loved one enjoyed. You don't have to spend time with everyone who invites you. You get to choose what to say yes to and what to say no to. Your energy and interest in holiday and family gatherings and events is likely to be different from how it was in the past with your loved one.

But don't automatically say no to everything and everyone. Don't isolate during the times when your loved one's memory is triggered most. As in the initial days of your grief, it can be important and healthy to spend some time alone to remember your loved one and care for your own heart. It is also important to connect with other people in meaningful ways during these times. Caring relatives and people in your church family can help provide distraction, support, and encouragement. And who knows? They may even help you experience moments of joy.

Some of your previous traditions you will want to continue. Doing so can be a way you remember and honor your loved one and continue to feel some connection with the person. But also choose to make some new memories around the holidays. Perhaps that means choosing some new decorations for your home, attending a new holiday church service, or volunteering in a way you had not previously.

Don't expect the holiday season to be easy. Knowing this in advance can help you determine who you will spend time with, when you will be alone, which traditions to continue, and what new memories you will make. Holidays only occur yearly, and the very fact that they are infrequent means you have fewer opportunities to experience the emotions connected with them. Use that to your advantage, especially in the first year or two. Say no to some of your usual responsibilities if you need to, and give yourself some extra time and grace to make it through the holiday season. This is just one more part of walking through the dark valley of grief.

Christmas was my husband's favorite holiday. Enjoying the Christmas tree and spending time with children and grandchildren was the highlight of the year for him. The first Christmas after his death was terribly hard for me. Putting up a Christmas tree felt emotionally overwhelming, so I didn't have one that year. The next year I wanted a Christmas tree again, and putting one up in my home was meaningful. It felt like I was in some way celebrating with Al again.

Remember that you get to choose. Don't ignore the holiday or anniversary, but you get to choose what old traditions or new memories to include.

Look beyond yourself.

Even while grieving, it's valuable to look beyond yourself. Grief is an intensely private emotion for most people, and during the journey through grief you're probably spending a lot of your energy looking inward, focusing on your own feelings. You need to do that to make progress on your journey, but focusing on yourself exclusively becomes depressing and unhealthy. Periodically raising your eyes from your own troubles and seeing those around you can be powerful mental and spiritual medicine.

The holiday season can be a valuable time to do this. If you have other family members, stretch yourself and help make the season special for them in some way. You may find it helpful to volunteer for some cause you or your loved one found meaningful—at your church, a hospital, a homeless shelter, an animal rescue organization, the Salvation Army, etc. Opportunities to volunteer abound during the holiday season. The idea is not to wear yourself out with work but to intentionally take your eyes off yourself and invest time in someone else, even if it's only briefly. Doing so will help you understand that you still have something to offer, that there are other people in need whom you can bless. It may be one of the first ways you experience moments of feeling good again after your loved one's death.

Honor your loved one's memory.

Special dates can provide important opportunities to honor your loved one's memory. You may choose to visit your loved one's resting place and leave something there. I visit Al's grave on Easter and sing resurrection hymns; it honors his memory and at the same time, it reminds me that cemeteries are only temporary housing. If you created a scrapbook or video to remember your loved one, you may wish to look at that again on birthdays or important anniversaries. You may want to write your loved one a letter again or journal about your memories of your time together.

Know too that you are likely to feel your loved one's loss much more acutely around these special dates than others around you do. Some friends or family who were important to your loved one may even forget about that special day. Don't take that personally. If a date is difficult for you and brings up an ambush of grief, it may be helpful to let a few people close to you know how you are struggling and ask for their support.

Take action if you get stuck in an ambush.

Most of the time an ambush of grief is like a wave; it rises in intensity and then lessens. Sometimes, however, a trigger or date will leave you stuck on that highway of overwhelming thoughts and feelings in your mind. If you find yourself stuck in an ambush, take some action. You don't have to drown.

You can revisit the healthy grieving steps discussed in chapters 3 and 4. Call a friend and ask to just talk. Write in your journal. Take a walk. Get a good night's sleep if possible. Spend some time reading Scripture passages that are meaningful. Get alone with God and pour out your heart to Him, and then stay there a little while and listen. You can get through this.

If you have thoughts of harming yourself, it's an emergency. Reach out for help right away. Call a family member, your pastor, someone in your grief group, your local crisis hotline, or your doctor. If you can't think of anyone else, just call 911. You don't have to do this alone.

Your loved one was an important part of your life. Countless experiences will remind you of the person and can function like a ramp onto the highway of innumerable thoughts and memories in your mind. The ambush of grief can feel overwhelming, but it is usually temporary.

Planning what to do when you feel ambushed by grief can help you move through those moments more effectively.

Important dates can be especially challenging for many going through grief. You don't have to say yes to everything; choose what old traditions to continue and what new memories to make. Lift your eyes from your own challenges and be a blessing to someone else, even if it's only for a brief moment. Finally, finding a special way to honor your loved one on special dates can be an important way to move forward on your journey through grief.

TWO STEPS FORWARD

1. How do you feel in body and mind when you experience an ambush of grief? Think of some things you can do next time you feel an ambush to move through the moment more effectively.

2. Are there any upcoming dates you are dreading? How can you plan ahead to make it through the day more meaningfully?

CHAPTER 11
CHOOSING TO HEAL

Earth has no sorrow that Heaven cannot heal.
—Thomas Moore, "Come Ye Disconsolate"

"TIME HEALS ALL wounds" is a myth. It's not simply the passage of time that brings healing. It's what you do with that time that counts.

I was talking with a physician friend who goes with a team from Samaritan's Purse into some of the worst disaster areas around the world. She was part of the first wave of medical personnel sent to the Mosul, Iraq, area as the battle to free that city from ISIS was underway. She returned to the same location six months later, and the difference was dramatic. On her second visit the medical team treated many people with old injuries that had never healed properly. One man had broken his leg months earlier. While he had been able to prevent infection with antibiotics, his leg had never been set and the bones had never fused. He was unable to walk because his lower leg was bent in an extra place, as if he had an extra knee. Surgery was necessary to give the bones a chance to heal.

As with a broken bone that goes untreated, it's possible for the wound of your grief to remain unhealed and become ugly, stinky, and infected. It's also possible for the wound to remain raw and open. Or you can let it heal. Yes, you will always have a scar. That will be a mark of your humanness and of the large and important place your loved one had in your life. But you don't have to let the wound paralyze you for the rest of your life. What you do today as you journey through this dark valley of grief will determine how grief affects your future.

In the early weeks and months after Al died, I was afraid I wouldn't "do grief right." I was worried I would neglect some important part of my grief work that would come back to sabotage me in the future. My fear was unnecessary. I learned that although there's no "right" way to grieve, there are ways to move forward that significantly aid the healing process.

In this chapter we'll talk about actively choosing to heal, what healing looks like, and some practical things you can do to help that process along. You can take steps to ensure that over time your grief wound neither becomes infected nor remains raw but heals.

Making the Choice to Heal

Making the choice to heal is different from either wallowing in grief or trying to plaster it over with spiritual platitudes. To heal, you must go through the dark valley. You don't park in the middle of the valley and set up residence there. You don't put one foot on the path and then shrink back.

Choosing to heal means you walk forward one step at a time. As messy, slow, inconsistent, and painful as it is, you must keep putting one foot in front of the other and walk through, not around, the dark valley.

To heal, you must "go there." You can't heal from a distance. Expecting to heal while keeping your grief at arm's length just doesn't work. That would be like a surgeon trying to operate on you over the phone. This can be one of the most inconvenient truths about grief that you will have to embrace. There are some ways in which healing really hurts. It may seem that the actions involved in choosing healing make your pain worse. But any worsening in your pain will be temporary. It's much like surgery. The procedure will leave you in pain, but it will allow healing to begin. Unfortunately, when it comes to grief, there's no anesthetic that can dull the pain. But there are ways to help the process along. That's why you're reading this book.

Choosing to heal means you walk forward one step at a time...through, not around, the dark valley of grief.

Healing doesn't happen in a moment. You can't "go there" all at once. It's too big, too much. And trying to do it all in one sitting would overwhelm your human system. Your brain wouldn't be able to process it all. The good news is that you don't have to. "Going there" is something you do one step at a time, just like all the other aspects of your grief journey.

Choosing to pursue healing is itself part of "going

there." Deciding to heal is not automatic. Not everybody chooses to pursue healing. Some decide to stay where they are, to set up residence in the dark valley. Again, you get no medals for speed, but choosing healing means quitting is not an option. It means you determine to keep walking even though you don't know all the details about what you're walking toward. You just decide that you can't stay where you are and you want to move forward into the future God has planned for you.

Choosing to pursue healing is something like choosing to eat. God makes a variety of food available, but that food doesn't enter your body and nourish your cells automatically. Unless you're an infant, you're responsible for knowing when you're hungry, finding appropriate food, preparing it, and taking it into your body. It's similar with healing. God has healing available, and there are many things that can help you experience that healing. But you're responsible to look for and choose appropriate means to help you in your healing journey; you must do the mental and spiritual "work" of chewing and swallowing. No magical activity, scripture, or step will move you from "wounded" to "healed." Like with meals, some activities, experiences, and truths will help you make greater progress through the grief journey than others. But you keep eating every day. You must keep choosing healing every day too.

What Healing Looks Like

Each person's healing is somewhat unique. It's as if God tailors your healing journey just for you. Yet there are some dimensions of healing that many believers have experienced and that you will likely experience also.

First, a word about what healing is **Healing** *not.* Healing does not mean you won't **means your** feel pain over your loved one's death. It **pain will** does not mean you will never experience an ambush of grief. It does not mean life **not define** will go back to the way it was before your **your future.** loved one died or that *you* will be like you were before. As much as you may wish for no more pain, that's not something you can expect in this world.

But healing does mean your pain will not define your future. Here are a few dimensions of healing that you can reasonably expect.

Your grief will be reframed.

Doing the work of grief means your feelings and memories will become integrated into the other dimensions of your life. The death of your loved one becomes something in your past rather than something in your present. Your loss becomes an important part of your experience but no longer defines you. The pain of your loss softens. It becomes something you carry with you, something you can access when you choose to rather than something that eclipses all else. The bleeding from your grief wound has stopped.

Healing means your bitterness, anger, confusion, or other emotions are in the past also. You've moved through the forgiveness process in whatever areas you needed to do so. You remember those feelings and still may experience them at times, but their sting is gone. Your grief work has allowed you to express those emotions and move past them. You've come to terms with the questions, even though some of them remain unanswered. You remember your loved one with all his or her quirks, strengths, and failures as an important part of your life. You can see the person reasonably honestly, and neither demonize nor idolize the individual. You've chosen to hold on to the positive memories of your loved one most strongly.

Through the healing process you also glean meaning from your grief experience. That does not necessarily mean you look for life lessons, although some people do learn lessons from their grief experience. It does mean your loved one's life and your experience of the person's death become integrated into your understanding of who you are, who God made you to be, and whatever bigger questions about the meaning of life have presented themselves to you. You're able to reflect on your grief journey as one who has been there rather than one who is in the middle of the dark valley right now. Your grief journey has deepened your perspective. Instead of seeing your loved one's death as something that was inflicted on you, you can embrace it as an experience you went through and grew through.

Remember that these are some aspects of healing that you can anticipate. Please don't add to your emotional burden by worrying about whether you're "on track." Experiencing and expressing your feelings in healthy ways, finding healthy means to remember your loved one, dealing with all the stuff, wrestling with God over the questions you have, and all the aspects of your grief work will bring you along this journey and to an increasing place of healing.

You begin to look toward the future.

We'll talk more about this in chapter 13. For now I'll just say healing means you grow into a new normal. I didn't like that concept at all when I began my grief work, and you may not either. When the initial waves of grief are overwhelming you, all your brain can process is today: what you are feeling, what you have to address, the next thing in front of you. That's normal, and that's why just doing the next thing is so important, especially early on. But as healing continues, you will be able to look a week into the future, then maybe a month. I still remember the first time I could begin to imagine a year ahead.

This is one of those areas to take slowly. Please don't try to imagine a year in the future during the initial months of your grief. You may look into the future and feel only panic and dread; that will pass. My neighbor experienced the death of her husband shortly before moving into the home next to me, and she expressed that for the first year all she felt was panic. This dynamic is one of the reasons it's wise to delay any decisions that aren't absolutely necessary until a year after your loved one's death. The process of healing to the point where you can look further into the future is likely to take a considerable period. Don't stress about this or force yourself to look ahead. Focus on your grief work, knowing that how far you can look ahead will expand as your healing process continues.

Your relationship with God deepens.

Healing also means your relationship with God is deepened and renewed. As we discussed in chapter 8, even a strong faith does not prevent questions and struggles during your grief journey. Healing means you have directed your questions to God. You've turned to Him for comfort and answers. You will never have all the answers, but healing means you have drawn closer to God as a result of wrestling with Him. Going through your grief journey may leave you with a limp, as Jacob had after wrestling with God (Gen. 32:25–31). But healing enables you to keep on walking, limp or not. Healing means you've chosen faith, and now your faith is more examined. Your relationship with God has more substance.

When any two people—friends, spouses, coworkers—go through something difficult together and get through to the other side, the relationship can be strengthened as a result. That can also happen with God as you find healing through your grief journey. You've gone through this terrible experience together. And through that experience, you discover what it means to have Him there with you and know He'll always be with you. It may be hard to imagine right now, but through your grief journey, your ability to trust God can actually increase as you experience what it's like for Him to be there for you even through your questioning, anger, and pain.

Steps Toward Healing

Healing is not like a baking a cake; there's no specific recipe that will guarantee a given outcome. Even more important, healing is not something you and I "do." Healing is something God through His Holy Spirit does in your heart, life, memory, mind, and emotions. Going back to the physical food analogy discussed earlier, you can't control every aspect of what the food you eat does when it enters your body. In the same way, you can't control how healing happens. But you can choose to believe in it, embrace it, pursue it, and trust God for it as you do what is within your power to do. You can choose to move toward healing.

Doing all the grief work discussed in this book is part of you embracing and pursuing healing. Here are a few specific ways you can intentionally continue that process.

Go there.

Several months after Al died, I took a few days off and went to a place we had enjoyed for one of our wedding anniversaries. I stayed in the same hotel, ate at the same restaurant, and walked on the same beach. I knew it would be painful, and it was! I also knew that going there would result in a tangible movement forward on my grief journey. I knew I had to "go there" in order to deal with some of my brokenness, confusion, and questions for God. I spent hours walking, journaling, praying, and thinking. Although my grief journey did not end there, that trip allowed me to take a huge leap forward in moving through the dark valley of my own grief.

In some way you will need to "go there." It's a principle in every healing process, whether for grief or for any other pain: abuse, trauma, addiction—the list goes on. Healing will not happen if you keep the pain at arm's length.

Find a way to go there. That may mean physically retracing some aspect of your relationship with your loved one, as I did, but it may not mean that. You can do this in many ways. Going through your loved one's things can be a means of "going there" if you take your time and feel the memories involved. Journaling is often a way of "going there." Talking about your loved one with others can be the same.

Because your brain cannot handle all these emotions at once, you will likely need to "go there" in various ways over many months. The point is to find ways to open the door into the deeper areas of your grief, whatever they are, and allow yourself to experience the feelings, thoughts, and memories that come. It's natural to shrink from "going there" because it will be painful. But healing happens as you take small steps to walk into and through the places where you dread to go.

Most importantly, take Jesus with you when you "go there." Intentionally invite Him to join you on the journey. Let your mind picture Him there beside you. What is His expression? How close is He to you? What is He doing? Is there anything you want to say to Him? Is He saying anything to you? This is not a theological exercise; it's a matter of inviting Jesus to minister to you where you need it most. In the deepest sense He is the only One who can truly go there with you. Invite Him to do so. You may be surprised at the moments of healing He brings. Go there with Him as often as you need to. He's ready!

Embrace gratitude.

While walking on the beach during my "going there" journey, I came to a place in my soul of profound gratitude. I had been intellectually grateful all along that God had blessed me with my husband and that God's presence was with me as I walked through grief. But as the sun baked my body and the waves washed my soul, I came to the place of actually *feeling* immense gratitude for Al's life. One of the big moments of healing Jesus brought me at that time was a profound sense of gratitude for how I had changed as a result of my marriage to Al. I sensed deeply that I would never have been able to do what God had called me to do were it not for Al's presence in my life. Our marriage and the life we shared taught me priceless things about love and relationships, and as a result I'm able to identify with and minister to others in the area of relationships in a way I never could have if I had not experienced marriage myself. Al's belief in the gifts God had blessed me with birthed a confidence in me that allows me to grow this ministry now. And although my pain and healing continued, coming to gratitude was an important turning point in my journey.

I encourage you to "look for the gratitude." Yes, intellectually expressing gratitude for the place your loved one had in your life is a good starting point. But keep going until you get to the place where you actually *feel* grateful—for your loved one's life, for who the person was to you, for how you are different as a result of knowing him or her, and for what having that individual in your life makes possible for your future. There's perhaps no greater way to honor your loved one than to embrace gratitude for who he or she was and is to you, and to hold on to that gratitude going forward.

Soak in His presence.

Ultimately, healing comes in God's presence. Inviting Jesus to "go there" with you is part of this. And you can look for other ways to soak in His presence. Keep going back to Scripture, prayer, and worship. You also may want to spend time in nature.

Early in your grief journey, your mind is not likely to process deeply or clearly; that's OK. Just keep going back into God's presence. Don't look at it as a time of activity or study or pressure. Look at it as a time of just being with Him. As you would expose your body to the sun while sunbathing, intentionally and repeatedly reveal your soul to the Son.

That's how you move toward the healing God has for you. Spending time in His presence gives Him the access He needs to minister healing to you. It's in His presence that your pain is comforted. It's there that He becomes the answer for your questions.

Like medical treatment for a serious illness, soaking in God's presence is not a one-and-done situation. You will need to spend time in His presence repeatedly. How do you do this? Find a place in nature that ministers to your soul and just go sit there. Find some worship music that seems to pull at something in your soul and play it often. Whatever helps you quietly enter into His presence, do that repeatedly. Just *be* with Him, and you will soon find you have moved toward healing.

Healing from the wounds of grief can feel impossible, especially because it's difficult to see anything in the future when overwhelmed by the pain of your loss. Healing doesn't happen simply because time passes; it comes because of what you do during that time. Choosing to pursue healing is an important step in getting there.

Healing will mean your pain is softened, and your memories and feelings about your loved one's death become integrated into the other parts of your life. And it will deepen your relationship with God. Intentionally look for the gratitude. Choose to "go there" into whatever wounds in your heart need healing, and invite Jesus to "go there" with you. Taking time to soak in the presence of God will help you move toward healing.

TWO STEPS FORWARD

1. Take a moment to honestly evaluate whether you have made the choice to embrace healing. What does that choice look like for you?

2. If you have made the choice to heal, what step(s) have you found most helpful in moving toward healing? After reading this chapter, are there any additional steps you will take?

CHAPTER 12
DEBUNKING MYTHS
ABOUT DEATH

I have come home at last! This is my real country!
I belong here. This is the land I have been looking
for all my life, though I never knew it till now.
—C. S. Lewis, *The Last Battle*

OUR MINDS CAN do funny things. Our senses and our thinking are the only ways we can process reality. They are also the only ways we can process God's truth. As believers, we have the Holy Spirit guiding us and are not limited to our own devices. But our minds are still the means through which we take in information. Because our human minds are curious and troubled by the loss of our loved ones, we naturally want to know more about death. We can hear stories of those who had near-death experiences and wonder, fear, or hope the accounts are true. There are plenty of theories, myths, and philosophies about what happens after death. But some of those ideas come from non-Christian worldviews, human reasoning, our own imaginations, or the enemy himself.

Some things we know about death, and some things we don't. When you're walking through the dark valley of grief, your mind may struggle to separate what's true from what isn't. It can be difficult to embrace the reality that God has not yet revealed everything we think we want to know about death and what happens thereafter. When we have many unanswered questions, in our humanness we can be prone to "filling in the blanks" where God's Word leaves some details unexplained. We want to know, "Where is my loved one?" We can want so much to know what our loved one experienced or is experiencing that we become vulnerable to beliefs not supported by Scripture, including things such as reincarnation and communication with the dead.

In this chapter we'll look at some of these ideas, beliefs, and philosophies from a biblical standpoint. This will not be a complete biblical exposition on the state of man in death. We will not theologically exhaust any of these questions. But I hope this discussion provides some perspective, some hope, and a framework to grapple with the sometimes competing and confusing ideas you may have heard about death.

As a starting place, let me point you to the underlying truths of the gospel that form the foundation of everything God has done, is doing, and will do in relation to humanity. These are things we know with certainty from Scripture. We know that human beings were created by God, are dependent on Him for life, and have earthly bodies formed from dust and that return to dust. Yet our Creator has made us for eternity. He has provided a way for us to live forever with Him, which is by embracing Jesus as our Lord and Savior because of His death and resurrection. We know that our time in this world is temporary, but God's kingdom will continue forever in a realm we can only partially now imagine. Those who make Jesus their Lord and Savior are assured that they will live eternally the

> **Death for the believer is not the end. It's the step between our life here and now and our life eternally.**

way God intended—fully alive in joy, peace, and communion with Him and others in the re-created earth when He makes all things new.

Death for the believer is not the end but only the in-between. It's the step between our life here and now and our life eternally. Is that step only one moment? What about the resurrection? What does "present with the Lord" in 2 Corinthians 5:8 (MEV) mean? Scripture tells us some things about death but not everything. Keeping the reality of what we know for certain in mind, let's address some of the challenging ideas and questions surrounding death from a biblical viewpoint.

Where Is My Loved One?

Only in eternity will we know everything we may think we want to know about what happens when someone dies. There are at least two word pictures in Scripture that may seem contradictory, and they have raised many questions for both theologians and believers.

Some passages portray those who have died as sleeping, not aware of anything, especially of what is going on here on earth. David said, "Among the dead no one proclaims your name. Who praises you from the grave?" (Ps. 6:5). Solomon wrote, "For the living know that they will die, but the dead know nothing; they have no further reward, and even their name is forgotten" (Eccles. 9:5). Jesus talked about death as sleep in stories such as those about Jairus' daughter and Lazarus (Luke 8:52; John 11:11–14). And Hebrews 11:40 says, "God had planned something better for us so that only together with us would they be made perfect." That verse seems to indicate that those who have died are not experiencing their reward but are waiting for us to join them so we can all experience it together.

This picture of death makes the resurrection "easier" to fit into the series of events our time-bound minds may imagine. Significant portions of the Christian church have taught that human beings who die simply sleep until Jesus' return when they will be raised to life again by the same power that raised Jesus from the dead and then enter heaven with Him.

Then there are those passages that paint a picture of one who believes in Jesus enjoying heaven immediately after death. Jesus spoke to the thief on the cross, "Today you will be with me in paradise" (Luke 23:43). In 2 Corinthians 5:1–8 Paul unpacks the phrase many of us love: "To be absent from the body [is] to be present with the Lord" (v. 8, MEV).

This passage does not indicate that those who are "with the Lord" have knowledge of anything happening here on earth or communication with those still walking this planet. Truthfully, this passage says essentially nothing about the state of those who are "with the Lord," such as their form, if any, or their consciousness, if any. Finally, John in Revelation speaks of seeing "the souls of those who had been slain because of the word of God" present in heaven before Jesus' return (Rev. 6:9–11). Are our loved ones enjoying heaven now? Bible scholars debate that question, and many church traditions affirm that believers who have died and are "present with the Lord" are conscious and experiencing all the joys of heaven while they await us to join them.

So which is it? Both pictures are in the Bible. When Scripture seems to contradict itself, the problem is with our understanding, not Scripture. I believe our problem is with our understanding of time. We naturally think in terms of sequence; one thing follows another. But Albert Einstein said that time is relative to the observer, and that events that appear sequential to one observer can appear simultaneous to another observer.[1] Einstein was no theologian, but his work does show that our human perspective is so limited. If human beings have been able to imagine time travel and different universes where time functions differently, who are we to limit God and how He deals with humanity? Death is entrance into eternity, so is it any surprise that we cannot fully understand the pictures God has given us of something we have not experienced?

What we do know for certain is that those who die who

believe in Jesus are preserved "present with the Lord." We can have absolute trust that the God who created us and who emptied all of heaven in the person of Jesus to bring us back to Himself has them safely in His hands. I'm not here to lobby for one interpretation of what happens when a person dies; there are things we don't know right now. But I am here to lobby for us to trust our questions to the One who has conquered death for all eternity.

Communicating With Deceased Loved Ones

This is one of the most common questions many going through grief wrestle with. In the early days and weeks after your loved one's death, you may experience times when you "feel" as though your loved one is with you. You may sense the person's presence. You may have dreams or other experiences when it seems your loved one is speaking to you. Some people feel as though their loved one's spirit is "hanging around," sharing parts of life with them, watching over them, or trying to communicate with them in some way. Things others may think of as coincidences may seem to affirm your loved one's presence to you.

At least a couple times in the initial weeks after Al's death, I had dreams in which I "saw" him and "heard" him communicate things to me. The experiences felt terribly real. I would have loved for them to *be* real. It's likely you may have similar experiences, though not everyone going through grief does. Some people have many more of these experiences than others do.

For centuries the church has generally interpreted Jesus'

story of the rich man and Lazarus as indicating that those who have died cannot travel between the heavenly realm and the earthly realm. (See Luke 16:19–31.) Intentionally seeking communication with the dead through séances or similar rituals is specifically forbidden in Scripture in passages such as Deuteronomy 18:10–12. Seeking to communicate with the dead puts one in danger of direct influence from Satan and his kingdom of darkness.

So what are we to think of the experiences of those who say they have sensed that their deceased loved one is present or communicating with them? It's important to remember that our experiences must not determine our theology. We must read Scripture for what it says, not for what we want it to say.

These experiences could be our own minds processing the loss of our loved one. The human mind is fully capable of doing such things. Based on Scripture, I believe this is the most likely explanation for most such experiences. And God is also certainly able to use our minds to bring comfort in unique ways. I know Al was not personally speaking to me in my dreams, but I can embrace a measure of comfort from the experience. I don't have to base my theology on that experience, however, or seek it again.

Can people feel the "spirit" of their loved one near them for a period after their death? I believe we must be very careful here. Again, we must base our theology on God's Word, not our experiences. The clearest teaching of Scripture is that our loved one's spirit is with the Lord, not here on earth.

Please keep in mind that it is possible for the enemy to craftily present experiences to your mind using demons that would appear like and sound like your loved one. If the experience is frightening, or especially if any message conveyed does not line up with God's Word, your most appropriate response would be to pray in the name of Jesus and intentionally enter God's presence in worship. You might say out loud, "Any spirit or influence not from God, be gone from me in Jesus' name! Heavenly Father, I need Your presence with me right here, right now."

Finally, there is no evidence in Scripture that our lives are directed or protected by loved ones who have died. That is a role God reserves for Himself through the ministry of angels and the Holy Spirit. Let God be God in your life, even during this journey through grief. Hold on to what Scripture does say, and trust God to handle the questions we don't have complete answers to. Your loved one lives in your memory. You are different because of the relationship you had with that person. That is the dimension in which your loved one continues to impact your life.

What About Near-Death Experiences?

Multiple stories exist of those who have "died" or been close to death for various periods (minutes, hours, sometimes longer) and then returned to life. Many of these stories are extremely vivid and convincing. Some incorporate medical or scientific support for the experience. Those who have been through such experiences describe them differently. Some talk about seeing or entering heaven, some about seeing hell, some about communicating with God or angels. Some are convinced they were given a message during their experience that they are to share. What are we to make of these stories? What, if anything, are we to believe as a result of hearing such claims?

Again, we must base our theology on Scripture, not on human experience. And as some Bible teachers have pointed out, these stories are all different. Therefore, they cannot all be portraying accurate information about what happens when a person dies.

Scripture tells us much about heaven. Jesus talked about it quite often. He also referred to hell numerous times. Bible scholars continue to wrestle with what *hell* means. What we can say for certain is that hell is a horrible place prepared for the devil and his angels (Matt. 25:41), and you don't want to be there! On the other hand, heaven is where God is. He wants you with Him. Jesus said, "I am going there to prepare a place for you" (John 14:2). Again, we know much about heaven but not everything. When John was writing Revelation, he struggled to find human language to describe the beauty and glory of the place. Old Testament writers struggled similarly. Paul is thought to be referring to himself when he wrote of a man who "was caught up to paradise and heard inexpressible things, things that no one is permitted to tell" (2 Cor. 12:4).

Let's be clear that we as humans do not know everything about what happens to a person at the moment of or after death. How God takes the human spirit and preserves it "present with the Lord" is beyond our ability to fully understand. Is it possible that the individuals who tell of these sometimes-beautiful experiences have been shown a part of reality that we cannot see? Yes. It's also possible that the human mind in the near-death state experiences things created by its own beliefs, memories, etc. I do not believe we necessarily need to dismiss these stories as false, but we must again base our theology on Scripture and not on human experience. If these stories are encouraging and spur you to develop a deeper relationship with God in the here and now, then God's Holy Spirit has used them for good.

Other Common Questions

Now for a few shorter questions that we can answer clearly from God's Word.

Does reincarnation happen?

Biblically we can answer this one clearly. Scripture says that "people are destined to die once, and after that to face judgment" (Heb. 9:27). Life here on earth is short, and we each get only one such life. How long each life will last we cannot know in advance; only God knows. But once that life here is over, it's over as far as earth is concerned. There is not another life on earth for anyone.

The idea of reincarnation comes from a non-Christian worldview. Whether the concept of reincarnation is appealing or frightening to you, the idea is clearly not biblical. A human being is not reborn as some other creature or in some other period of history.

Should we pray for or be baptized for the dead?

This question sometimes arises from this comment Paul made: "Now if there is no resurrection, what will those do who are baptized for the dead? If the dead are not raised at all, why are people baptized for them?" (1 Cor. 15:29). This is the only verse in Scripture where this is mentioned, and history does not offer clarification on any specific practice that could be characterized as "baptism for the dead" in the early Corinthian church.

Going back to what we know to be true, salvation comes through one's own faith in Jesus. Romans 10:9 declares, "…that if you confess with your mouth Jesus is Lord, and believe in your heart that God has raised Him from the dead, you will be saved" (MEV). Whatever Paul is talking about in 1 Corinthians 15:29, being baptized for someone who has died does not cause them to be saved or alter their eternal destiny.

Paul's comment in 1 Corinthians comes during his defense of the reality of Jesus' resurrection and therefore our resurrection in the future as believers in Him. His comment may well be simply rhetorical. Whatever practice he is referencing, he neither condemns nor condones. It's one of those biblical statements we can leave a question mark nearby and base our theology on the primary point Paul was making. No, the Bible does not direct us to pray or be baptized for the dead, and certainly not for the purpose of effecting the deceased person's salvation.

Can a person repent and accept Jesus after death?

I earlier mentioned Hebrews 9:27, "People are destined to die once, and after that to face judgment." Numerous other scriptures also make it clear that our eternal destiny is determined by the choice we make during this life to believe in Jesus as our Lord and Savior. Peter preached, "And everyone who calls on the name of the Lord will be saved" (Acts 2:21). Paul told the Philippian jailer, "Believe in the Lord Jesus, and you will be saved—you and your household" (Acts 16:31). As one of my theology professors used to say at funerals, "My job is not to preach your loved one into either heaven or hell; those decisions were made during their lifetime."

There is no evidence in Scripture that one's eternal destiny can be changed after death. Once death has occurred, repentance and salvation are no longer possible.

But remember that God is patient, "not wanting anyone to perish, but everyone to come to repentance" (2 Pet. 3:9). He's looking for a way to save as many as possible, including your loved one. You and I do not know what happened in our loved ones' minds and hearts in the moments surrounding their death. While their eternal destiny became sealed at that point, we can be certain that God knows whether they called out to Him. And He can be trusted to deal rightly with our loved one and with us.

Unanswered Questions

As with the *why* questions, the questions about death can best be satisfied when you turn them into *who* questions.

Those things about death, salvation, resurrection, eternal life, heaven, etc. that the Bible talks about clearly we can be certain of. There are other things that we can speculate about, but we must never confuse our speculation with the truth. Some of the things we wonder about we will only fully understand when we experience eternity for ourselves. In the meantime we can trust in the One who holds our loved ones in His hands and holds our future.

Imagine you're a parent. (Perhaps you are.) You plan a vacation to the beach, and you are certain your children will be thrilled with the experience. You do your best to describe the ocean, the gulls, the sand, the breeze, and the sound of the waves. But your children can't comprehend what they haven't yet seen and experienced for themselves. Pictures, stories, and reassurance aren't enough to let your children know what it will be like. But your children would be right to trust you when you assure them it will be wonderful.

It's the same with God and eternity. We imagine all kinds of problems, questions, and uncertainties. We worry or wonder about things that are not confusing at all to God. Whatever His Word does not speak to directly, we can trust that He has under control. And by knowing in whom we trust, our hearts can be satisfied.

Many people wonder about death. We believe intuitively that there is something beyond what we see and experience in this life, and God's Word confirms this is true. What exactly happens at the time of death is something we can only partially understand. We can be assured that God is well able to preserve those who belong to Him in a state of being "present with the Lord," and that to be in His presence is glorious for our loved ones, whatever that looks like between now and when we join them in eternity. We can also be assured that God is looking for any possible way to save our loved ones, and He can be trusted with those decisions.

Scripture indicates that after death our loved ones are not communicating with us or involved in our lives here. Details of the afterlife described by those who claimed to have had near-death experiences may or may not be true. But we can trust God's Word that heaven and the new earth will be more wonderful than we can fully imagine. And we can safely trust our unanswered questions to the One who is in charge.

TWO STEPS FORWARD

1. Perhaps this chapter has challenged some of your beliefs around death. If so, write about your thoughts in your journal. And then take those thoughts to God in prayer.

2. How well are you trusting God with the things about death you don't completely understand? In your journal write a prayer to God about this.

CHAPTER 13
MOVING FORWARD WITHOUT YOUR LOVED ONE

To live in hearts we leave behind
Is not to die.
—THOMAS CAMPBELL, "HALLOWED GROUND"

LIFE WILL NEVER be the same. That doesn't automatically mean your life will be worse; it only means it will be different. In the midst of your journey through the valley of grief, it may seem impossible to imagine how there could be anything positive in your future. As one who is still walking this journey, let me offer you some hope. As challenging as it may be to do so, you can come to embrace a new normal. In that new normal your loved one will be with you in memory though not physically present. Embracing that new normal doesn't happen quickly, but you can get there.

You've experienced this at other times in your life. As a child you moved from one grade to another, then from elementary or middle school to high school, perhaps from singleness to marriage to parenthood. Each new normal may sometimes be challenging. It may feel very uncomfortable for a while. But not everything about the new normal will be bad. Coming to embrace a life without your loved one's physical presence will happen in a similar way. Moving forward after the loss of a loved one can be a difficult transition, but it is possible.

I have met people who lost a spouse or child years ago, but they still live as if the loss occurred just a week ago. If that's the case for you, know that you are not alone. Growing into a new normal is not easy. But if a year, two years, three years have passed and you are not sensing some new normal gradually developing in your life, get some help. Being stuck in grief does not mean there's something irreparably wrong with you; it just means you need some wise and caring assistance to get unstuck.

It's been said that friends, money, and a sense of purpose determine much about how a person develops a new normal. If the loved one who died provided your primary source of income, a sudden lack of money can add a lot to your stress and make your grief journey more complicated. If you have no close friends currently, it can take more-than-usual energy to grow forward. And without a sense of purpose it will be difficult to feel any motivation to grow into a new normal. It's possible to overcome any or all these challenges. If these are factors for you, I encourage you to be even more intentional about doing your grief work and getting some help if you are not making progress.

Your ability to move forward without your loved one's physical presence will develop slowly. In this chapter we'll explore some of the elements that can be important in this part of your journey.

Carrying Your Loved One With You

Some who are going through the grief journey feel as though moving forward in any way would mean they are dishonoring or disrespecting their loved one who died. You may, perhaps unconsciously, feel that experiencing any happiness or taking any positive action without your loved one's physical presence would somehow mean you didn't love the person enough. Remaining miserable and stuck in your grief somehow seems proof of what your loved one means to you.

Intellectually you may realize that such thoughts are not wise or reasonable. They're common human thoughts, but let me urge you to challenge those thoughts if you have them. If you could imagine your loved one now, he or she would want you to be happy. The person would want you to move forward with your life in some way. Perhaps your loved one even said something to you to that effect if he was aware the end of his time on earth was near.

Moving forward does not dishonor our loved ones. Doing so may actually be one of the most important ways we can value, honor, and respect who they were and the impact they had on us. It may be helpful to evaluate some specific ways in which you can intentionally carry your loved one with you as you move forward. Your relationship with your loved one is not over; it's just that now your relationship is one of memory and legacy instead of physical presence.

Moving forward does not dishonor our loved ones. Doing so may actually be one of the most important ways we can honor them and the impact they had on us.

It can be helpful to intentionally develop that new relationship of memory. I mentioned previously that during the time I spent alone with God at the beach early in my grief journey, I came to feel immense gratitude for who my husband had been to me, how our marriage had changed me, and what that would make possible now. That has become a significant part of my own journey to move forward. I have come to appreciate that our marriage, though much shorter than either of us would have wanted, allowed me to develop an understanding and appreciation of relationship and intimacy that I would not have had any other way. That very understanding has since become one of the primary ways in which I am able to minister to others. People struggling with intimacy or marriage issues often seek me out, ask me questions, read things I've written, or request help in these areas. Each and every time I help someone in the area of relationships or marriage, I am carrying my husband with me. Who he was to me comes out in almost everything I say and write. Without him in my life for those years, I would have no ability to do what I'm doing now.

As you move forward, you can carry your loved one with you in some way as well. Who you became as a result of your loved one's investment in your life impacts your skills, understanding, resilience, courage, ability to love, and a hundred other characteristics. Embracing those things is part of honoring your loved one. Some people honor their loved one by investing themselves in a cause that was or would have been meaningful to their loved one. Others, after an appropriate time of healing, pour themselves into helping others as a way of expressing the love they are not able to physically show their loved one now.

You have many choices about how to use your stored memories of your relationship with your loved one. When you face a situation in which you previously would have relied on your loved one's input or support, or when you are feeling emotional again over your loss, intentionally remembering your loved one can help you access that same sense of input and support. When I face a challenge in ministry, I sometimes do that by thinking about all my husband taught me about media. There are likely to be many times when you will want to bring out the physical reminders you have created of your loved one, such as a scrapbook or video. Bringing your loved one to mind and reviewing the personal items you've chosen to save can help you choose the best memories to hold on to and continue to experience the positive aspects of your loved one's impact on your life.

Doing your grief work will help you discover things

about yourself you didn't know before, including ways in which your loved one impacted you and others. Taking the time to examine your loved one's legacy in your own heart can help you understand how you wish to carry the person's memory forward as you move with God into this next season of your life. It's worth intentionally thinking about that. Doing so may be the greatest way to honor your loved one and the role that person played in your life.

At times in this book I have alluded to scenarios in which a person's relationship with a loved one who died was traumatic. Conflict, abuse, addiction, or other serious issues can complicate a person's life and the lives of those around that individual. What then? It is still possible to do your grief work, explore your feelings, take Jesus with you into the places of your pain, and invite God's comfort and presence to bring healing to your heart. You are still different because of your relationship with your loved one. Perhaps you need even more healing now than someone else facing loss. Even if your loved one's life brought you enormous pain, your grief work can bring you to the place where the memory of the trauma loses its sting and you become able to move forward into the next season of what God has for you.

God's Purpose for You

God cares about you in your grief. He sees you, weeps with you, understands you, and is patient with you. As much as He cares about you right now, He also sees the future that you probably struggle to see right now. He sees who you are becoming as a result of your journey through this dark valley of grief. He knows the ways you are growing. He appreciates that, as was the case with Jacob in the Old Testament, you will have a limp as you move forward. (See Genesis 32:25, 31.) He knows the scar forming in your soul as a result of your grief and the ways in which this journey is changing you.

Remaining stuck in grief is like saying you know better than God that your future without your loved one is meaningless. If you're still breathing, God has something yet for you to do.

More than anything else, God knows what your future will be. He knows what this next season of your life can become and the ways in which even your grief journey is preparing you for what is yet to be. Please hear me: God did not take your loved one home in order to teach you something so you could fulfill some purpose of His. But God does have a miraculous way of turning what would otherwise be harmful, including your loved one's death, into something valuable for His kingdom and meaningful for you.

Remaining stuck in grief is, in one sense, saying you know better than God that your future without your loved one is meaningless. If you're still breathing (and you are or you wouldn't be reading this), God has something yet for you to do. It may or may not be something you suspect right now. It may be something seemingly small in human eyes but that will make a significant difference for God's kingdom. It may be something that directly relates to the relationship you shared with your loved one, or it may be something different. But you can be certain that you are not still alive by accident. When the darkness feels like more than you can see beyond and you think you want to leave this world and be with your loved one, remember that God still has something for you to do.

Very near the end of Paul's life he wrote his letter to the Philippians, where we find this:

> For to me, to live is Christ and to die is gain. If I am to go on living in the body, this will mean fruitful labor for me. Yet what shall I choose? I do not know! I am torn between the two: I desire to depart and be with Christ, which is better by far; but it is more necessary for you that I remain in the body. Convinced of this, I know that I will remain, and I will continue with all of you for your progress and joy in the faith, so that through my being with you again your boasting in Christ Jesus will abound on account of me.
>
> —PHILIPPIANS 1:21–26

Can you see Paul's point? Although a big part of him wanted to die and be present with the Lord, he determined to remain here on earth as long as God had a purpose for him to fulfill. I have come to the same conviction. Although going through each day as a widow is difficult, I'm both satisfied and convinced that I'll be here as long as

God needs me here and not a moment longer. Some days it's not easy to see that purpose. But like Paul, you and I can choose to believe that God still has a purpose for us and continue to walk forward.

In the early period after your loved one's death all you can see is right now, this moment of pain. Embracing the reality that God still has a purpose for you involves being able to look a little further into the future. That ability increases as you keep walking through the valley of your grief. You come to see God as someone who comforts you, yes, but who also supports you as you fulfill a purpose greater than yourself.

You may be at the point in your grief journey where you're beginning to believe God still has something for you to do, but you don't have a clue what that could be. You feel as though you would find your grief somewhat less painful if you could only understand a little more of what God's purpose for you might be. Just appreciating that reality means you are looking further into the future than you could at first. That's a healthy point in your grief journey.

Embracing and fulfilling God's purpose for this next season of your life is not something to stress about or become frantic or desperate over. It's something that you usually come to understand slowly, over time. It's something you grow into. God's purpose for you always involves someone or something beyond yourself.

Embracing your purpose first means investing in your personal relationship with Him. As we have discussed, your very grief journey can be a vehicle to deepen the

THE CHRISTIAN'S JOURNEY THROUGH GRIEF

intimacy you have with God. Invest regularly in entering His presence, learning to listen, and allowing Him to do what He wants to do in your heart. That's the only way fulfilling your purpose becomes possible.

As you keep walking this journey, at some point you will sense God directing your focus upward, outward, and beyond yourself. You will start to see others who need something you have. Someone else's hurt will burden you, and you will wonder how God might want you to come alongside that person. You will feel the Holy Spirit impressing you to reach out to help someone and give something of yourself. As you take those steps that seem both difficult and small at first, you will find even more healing for your own grief journey and begin to embrace God's purpose for the next season of your life.

Risking Loving Again

You are grieving because you loved. No love, no grief. And one of the most challenging parts of the grief journey for many is considering loving again.

For some who lost a spouse, loving romantically again can become a rebound, a way to try to short-circuit the pain and fill the place their spouse occupied in their life. Some who lost a child may think of having another child, hoping to fill the place of the one who died. Intellectually you may realize that doing something like this is not wise. Imagining that such decisions mean you are loving again does not make them real love. It's not fair for either you or the person you're trying to love. You're able to consider loving again when you've progressed enough in your grief journey that any new relationship or child can be about *this* relationship and not about the one you lost. For most people that process takes a year or two at least.

You may also shrink from loving again because love is a risk. You may feel like keeping your heart protected, closed, insulated. Loving in any way seems as though it would require more of you than you could possibly give. C. S. Lewis wrote about that.

> To love at all is to be vulnerable. Love anything, and your heart will be wrung and possibly be broken. If you want to make sure of keeping it intact, you must give your heart to no one, not even to an animal. Wrap it carefully round with hobbies and little luxuries; avoid all entanglements; lock it up safe in the casket or coffin of your selfishness. But in that casket—safe, dark, motionless, airless—it will change. It will not be broken; it will become unbreakable, impenetrable, irredeemable.[1]

Nobody can or should be allowed to tell you if or when it's time to risk loving again. But it's important to know that doing so is not dishonoring to your loved one. God loves each human being individually, yet He loves us all overwhelmingly. His love for you is not diminished by His love for me or anyone else. That's the nature of love. Love is not a finite commodity where loving one person means you have less with which to love another. (Don't misunderstand this to imply that love in marriage need not be exclusive.) Rightly understood, love multiplies itself.

Opening your heart to love again provides meaning and helps you move forward in the purpose God has for you.

Those principles about love don't apply only to romantic love. But when it comes to romantic love, there are some special considerations. Let me offer a few suggestions. You will know you are perhaps ready to think about loving romantically again when:

- Your grief journey is something in your past rather than something in your present.

- You have learned to live as a single person and have come to find your life's meaning in connection with God and others outside of a romantic relationship.

- You have come to terms with living alone, even if you don't like it.

- You are able to consider a relationship not in terms of what a person can give to you but what you have to give someone else.

- You can experience times of joy even though your previous spouse is not there.

- You are giving of yourself to others in meaningful ways that have nothing to do with romantic love.

- Though ambushes of grief occur at times, they do not define your life.

These are some of the indicators that you may be ready to consider a relationship that is about *this* person and not about your former spouse.

In a larger sense loving again has to do with God's purpose for the next season in your life. Here I'm not talking about romantic love at all. Loving again in this sense means life is not all about you. It means you are beginning to seek ways to give to others the substance with which God has filled you. That may be through nurturing people in your family, expanding your vocational/work abilities, or volunteering at church or some other setting. It means that, like Paul, you're paying attention to what "is more necessary for you" (Phil. 1:24)—which is how others can be blessed by what you have to offer—and you are finding healthy ways to offer it.

Loving again in some way is a measure of the healing God has brought you in your journey through grief. Move forward slowly. If your spouse was the loved one you lost, that may or may not mean you will seek romantic love again. But as God brings your heart to the place where it's ready, loving again in the sense of looking beyond yourself will be one of the things that makes this next season of your life meaningful. And it may become one of the ways in which you honor the love you shared with your loved one and carry the person's memory forward.

Moving forward without your loved one physically present is not easy. Even thinking about doing so is usually difficult.

Most people cannot do this during the early stages of their grief journey, but growing into a new normal is possible. That new normal is not necessarily a negative experience, but it will be different. Intentionally thinking about how you will choose to carry your loved one's memory forward with you can help make this transition meaningful.

As your grief journey continues, you will become increasingly able to look beyond today. Embracing the reality that God still has a purpose for you will become more and more important. That purpose may even be made fuller by the memory of your loved one and the relationship you shared with that individual. And growing into that new normal will mean risking loving again in some way—not to replace the love you had for your loved one, but to express the multiplication of the love God has blessed you with. Learning to again look beyond yourself and give to others is perhaps the best expression of pursuing God's purpose for you in this next season.

TWO STEPS FORWARD

1. What positive aspect of your loved one's legacy will you carry forward? In what way will you do so?

2. What are you coming to understand about the purpose God still has for you?

CHAPTER 14
THE HOPE OF HEAVEN

If you're not allowed to laugh in heaven, I don't want to go there.
—Martin Luther

My home is in Heaven. I'm just traveling through this world.
—Billy Graham

THERE'S ONLY ONE way to make it through the valley of grief, and that is to embrace the hope of heaven. One way to translate Romans 8:24 is: "For we were saved by means of hope." Being able to look forward to the future God has planned, has promised, and is well able to deliver is truly what makes our grief different from "others who have no hope" (1 Thess. 4:13, MEV). I sometimes wonder how people without this hope even survive the experience of grief.

The entire experience of walking through the valley of grief could be described as a journey from focusing your mind on your excruciating loss to focusing it on the hope of heaven. In that process even the overwhelming pain of grief becomes "our light and momentary troubles" when compared with "an eternal glory that far outweighs them all" (2 Cor. 4:17). The pain of grief is not removed by this hope, but it is put in perspective.

Perspective really does change everything. Imagine being stranded in a small boat during a storm, waves crashing over you, threatening to drown you. You're soaked and terrified. Suddenly a helicopter hovers above you, a rescuer plunges into the water beside you, a basket is lowered, and you are lifted to safety. Your perspective suddenly goes from water level to hundreds or thousands of feet above the waves. From the window of the helicopter speeding off with you in it, the light catching the waves appears brilliant and beautiful. You can now focus on more than gasping for your next breath as fear is replaced with relief and hope.

That's what the hope of eternity can do for you in your grief. That's what a change in perspective can do to your pain. That's what being saved by hope feels like. That hope may not overtake you as quickly as a helicopter extracting you from a stranded boat, but it can become just as certain of a lifeline. It *will* come if you keep walking.

Heaven and the New Earth

No section in a chapter of a book can come close to adequately describing what heaven is like. Jesus talked often about both heaven and "the renewal of all things" (Matt. 19:28), as do many of the New Testament writers. Ever since then many saints have tried to put into words the beauty, joy, and glory of heaven with only partial success. Our human language cannot do it justice. And yet heaven will not be the end. God has promised to make all things new, including earth. That's where the New Testament ends—not in heaven, but right here on earth with everything re-created. Only then will God's eternal purposes for creation and for us be fulfilled.

This truth gives all humanity great reason to hope. But let's look specifically at some of what the promise of heaven and the new earth means for us who are going through the valley of grief.

Our hope is in a real place.

One thing you cannot escape noticing throughout the New Testament is that Jesus and all who followed Him believed heaven to be as real as the things we can see with our physical eyes, perhaps even more so. Jesus spoke of preparing a place for us there, a home in His Father's house (John 14:1–3). He spoke of heaven as a place with rewards, books, a banquet, treasures, a city, and angels that pass between here and there. He spoke of His Father as being in heaven and Himself as coming from heaven and going back there. Heaven is certainly not some ethereal place where disembodied spirits play harps all day. Taking Jesus' words at face value, one would have to conceptualize heaven as a realm we cannot see now but that is at least as real as our present world, only perfect and permanent. Paul and John both were allowed glimpses of heaven, and they were overwhelmed by the experience.

Think of those who were persecuted and even killed in the early centuries after Jesus walked the earth and those who are still willing to give up their lives in places where believing in Jesus is physically dangerous today. Would so many gladly endure persecution and even death if they weren't as convinced as Jesus was that the eternity God has promised us is real? Even before Jesus came to earth, Abraham by faith looked "forward to the city with foundations, whose architect and builder is God" (Heb. 11:10). Heaven is very real.

Paul wrote about us having bodies in heaven that are different from the ones we have here, bodies that are themselves permanent and not subject to sickness or death. (See 1 Corinthians 15:42–44.) He wrote of us having a "spiritual body." Perhaps a more correct translation is that we will have a "spirit-empowered body." This is not meant to suggest our eternal bodies will not have substance. We may not understand exactly how a spiritual body will look, but we have every reason to believe our heavenly bodies will be in form very much like what we know now. God created humankind in His image, so we are already very much like Him, with hands, feet, eyes, and all the other such things we think of as part of the body. We will have eyes capable of tears that God Himself will wipe away. We will have feet to walk through the gates of the New Jerusalem, and a mouth and senses to enjoy eating from the tree of life. (See Revelation 21–22.) Our bodies will be re-created to reflect what God originally intended.

The first two chapters of Genesis talk about how "God

created the heavens and the earth" (Gen. 1:1). The last two chapters of Revelation talk about how God re-creates "a new heaven and a new earth" (Rev. 21:1). God's plan is not thwarted—detoured perhaps, but not thwarted. And finally it all comes to pass. John describes a city with gates and foundations. There are rivers and trees with leaves and fruit. Taking Jesus' frequent talk about "the regeneration" together with John's description in Revelation, the new earth is what God had intended all along. It's Eden restored—physical bodies, relationships, nature, health, and joy all made gloriously perfect, along with God's physical presence forever with us here on earth.

And about those tears. We have sorrow and weep now. But picture being in the new earth. God Himself, the One who created you and gave His Son for you, is now walking up to you, putting His arm around you. Then with His eternal hand, "He will wipe every tear from [your] eyes" (Rev. 21:4). I've read that verse for years, but it means so much more to me now.

I believe in part this also means our tears will not be wiped away before eternity. We can receive true comfort, healing, and growth here in this life, yet tears will still be a reality for us. But the day will come when God Himself, the One who stands at the center of the universe and has been planning this day since before time began, will take His heavenly, golden handkerchief and wipe your tears away with a touch so gentle, lovely, and overwhelming that you will never need to cry again. And the meaning behind this picture is that not only will He wipe the tears away from your eyes but from your heart as well.

Of course, everything wonderful will be a part of eternity with God: adventure, excitement, fulfillment, healing, peace, growth, learning, intimacy, romance, accomplishment, satisfaction, creativity, abundance, true love, and every other wonderful gift you can imagine. And everything horrible will never, ever show up again. Pain, shame, embarrassment, loss, confusion, inhibition, sadness, fear, worry, lack, trauma, and most of all death will be eliminated forever.

The day will come when God Himself will take His heavenly, golden handkerchief and not only wipe the tears away from your eyes but from your heart as well.

Our personalities in heaven

Some people wonder if they and their loved ones will be able to recognize one another in eternity. The Bible indicates that we will. Jesus' disciples were promised a role in governing "the twelve tribes of Israel" (Matt. 19:28). That would seem to imply the disciples would have similar personalities and even physical characteristics to what they had when Jesus spoke those words. Many Bible scholars interpret Paul's statement in 1 Corinthians 13:12 in a similar way: "Then I shall know fully, even as I am fully known." We will both know others and be known for who we really are, more completely than in any human relationships we have now.

What we do here on earth now has carryover into our experience in eternity. In the parable of the talents in Luke 19, the servants who diligently invested what they were entrusted with were given significant authority when the king returned (vv. 17, 19). Jesus spoke about storing up "treasures in heaven" (Matt. 6:20). He often said that what we do here will impact our reward in heaven. This reward is not salvation. But somehow in God's economy our time here on earth is not wasted. The things we learn, the choices we make, the skills we develop, and the things we invest in God's kingdom now affect what we will be doing in eternity.

Getting to Heaven

We touched on this earlier in this book, but it deserves another brief discussion here. One cannot read Scripture without being convinced that some human beings will not be in heaven. But God makes abundantly clear that His desire is for each person to be saved. "The Lord is not slow in keeping his promise, as some understand slowness. Instead he is patient with you, not wanting anyone to perish, but everyone to come to repentance" (2 Pet. 3:9). The parables of the lost sheep, lost coin, and lost (prodigal) son in Luke 15 show God as One who does everything possible to save every single human being.

And yet He does not force anyone into heaven or the re-created new earth. Jesus is pictured in Revelation 3:20

as knocking, waiting for a response from the heart. And when a person does respond, He rejoices. He is looking for any possible reason to save as many as possible—you, me, and our loved ones. The response He is looking for is not for us to try harder, or grovel, or profess a certain religious affiliation. None of those things matter when it comes to salvation. He's looking for someone to say yes. And every single time, without exception, when someone says yes, He says yes in return. As Romans 10:13 declares, "Everyone who calls on the name of the Lord will be saved."

What does saying yes look like? Romans 10:9 says, "If you declare with your mouth, 'Jesus is Lord,' and believe in your heart that God raised him from the dead, you will be saved." There's nothing anyone can do to earn their way into heaven. Treating other people right, doing penance for the wrongs you've done, giving money to good causes or the church, keeping yourself out of trouble, being born with the right pedigree—none of that makes a bit of difference. And God won't check your weight, smoking status, bank account, or political or church activities on your way into the New Jerusalem. The only thing that matters is that you said yes to His knock on the door of your heart.

And that's the only thing that matters about your loved one as well. Although the legacy our loved ones leave on earth is determined by their behavior during their lifetime, what matters when it comes to where they spend eternity is their heart's posture toward God. And once again, if you're unsure of how your loved one stood with God at the time of the person's death, remember that only God knows what transpired in the last moments of your loved one's life here on earth. I believe all of us will be surprised at some of those whom we will meet in heaven.

Since we're on the subject, I cannot close this book without asking you to make sure you have said yes to Jesus' knock on your own heart's door. Heaven is too wonderful to miss. When God re-creates the new earth we will finally be able to fully experience everything we were created for. Regardless of what may happen during the remainder of your life here, don't miss your chance to let God come personally to you and wipe away the tears from your eyes—and your heart. I want to meet you in heaven and the new earth. And I pray you meet your loved one there as well.

Finding Hope in the Midst of Pain

The journey through the valley of grief is possible because of hope. Sometimes that hope seems hard to grasp, and it seems as though the waves of sadness will drown you. Know that you are not the first one to go through this valley, and you are not the only one going through it right now. As dark and hopeless as things may appear, you can be certain that what you see and feel right now is not all there is.

Knowing Jesus and connecting with a community of faith makes a difference here and now. But as Paul said, "If only for this life we have hope in Christ, we are of all people most to be pitied" (1 Cor. 15:19). However good this life may be, it's never enough. As long as your loved one lived, it wasn't long enough. Even as good as it is to know Jesus here, it's not enough. Only with the hope of heaven and the new earth, only with the reality of eternity, can your soul ever find satisfaction or gather the courage to go on. Only with our eyes regularly returning to the view of eternity can this life be meaningful. Let us fix "our eyes on Jesus, the pioneer and perfecter of faith. For the joy set before him he endured the cross, scorning its shame, and sat down at the right hand of the throne of God" (Heb. 12:2). If Jesus had to keep His eyes on eternity to make it, how much more you and I will have to do the same.

Grief is supposed to hurt; it's the price of love. Death was not part of how God originally designed things to be, and in His universe it's not normal. Your pain now is a mark of how wrong things have gone here on earth and of how much sin has messed everything up. But even in the middle of your pain, you can choose to embrace hope.

Some days the waves of sadness, loneliness, hopelessness, anxiety, panic, or pain will threaten to overwhelm you. Look for the waves of hope. The reality of heaven, the absolute certainty that God will set all things right and that He will wipe all tears from your eyes when He makes all things new, can wash over you too. Don't deny or ignore the waves of pain; often you will have to ride those waves and let them crash on the shores of your soul. But at the same time, choose to also ride the waves of hope.

When you need a moment of hope, call a friend. Cry out for God's presence. And read again Paul's declaration about the death of death:

For the trumpet will sound, the dead will be raised imperishable, and we will be changed. For the perishable must clothe itself with the imperishable, and the mortal with immortality. When the perishable has been clothed with the imperishable, and the mortal with immortality, then the saying that is written will come true: "Death has been swallowed up in victory."

"Where, O death, is your victory? Where, O death, is your sting?"

—1 CORINTHIANS 15:52–55

Even so, come, Lord Jesus!

TWO STEPS FORWARD

1. How does looking forward to the time when God will wipe away all your tears help you make it through the dark valley of grief?

2. Write in your journal about what you are looking forward to in heaven and the new earth.

A FINAL WORD

YOUR LOVED ONE'S memory is precious. Priceless. So is your heart. And so is your grief journey. As you keep walking through this dark valley, the light will slowly begin to shine again. Welcome those moments when you can sense the light beginning to return.

Although you are the only one who can take one step after another through this dark valley, you do not have to make the journey alone. Intentionally look for the people you can reach out to who can come alongside you in various ways. And most of all, invite Jesus to walk this journey with you. He will not leave you alone.

Your tears right now are precious too. Let them flow. You can make it through this journey one day at a time. And along the way, hold on to the certain hope of the coming day when God will wipe all your tears away. It will be worth it.

And if I don't meet you here on earth, I will hope to see you in eternity.

ACKNOWLEDGMENTS

THE AUTHOR'S NAME on a book cover gives the impression that the author is the source of said book. But that belies the team effort that is necessary for a book such as this to come into being. Especially with a book as personal as this, drawn out of my own grief journey, others become indispensable in bringing this message into your hands.

First, I want to thank Joe Champion, senior pastor at Celebration Church, and Anne Eppright, GriefShare leader, for your words, thoughts, hugs, and care after the death of my husband, Al. Though I knew all the stuff already, your Christian love and support was like water to my soul as I walked through my own dark valley of grief.

Thank you to Dr. Edward Decker, my former professor at ORU, for challenging me on a few theological points in an early draft of this book, resulting in a presentation that is cleaner and truer to Scripture. You have always stretched me to be better.

Thank you to Debbie Marrie, vice president of product development at Charisma House, for seeing what this book could become, and to Adrienne Gaines for your hard work in nurturing this manuscript into something worthy of publication. Thank you to Lucy Kurz, Maureen Eha, Margarita Henry, SueLee Charron, Nicole Ponder, Rachel Sammons, Ann Mulchan, and the entire team at Charisma House for all your efforts in bringing this book into the world.

A huge thank-you to Karen Neumair, COO at Credo Communications and my illustrious literary agent, for believing in me and this project, and for talking me down off the dangerous cliffs any author encounters from time to time.

My heartfelt personal thanks to Woodley Auguste, Omar Galarza, and Mady Galarza for your friendship and listening ears. You've seen and heard me during some of my most painful moments, and you've loved me anyway. And for us as a team, this is only the beginning.

To my husband, Al Tanksley, I love you and miss you every day! Although you cannot read these words, because of you I know what it is like to be cherished as a woman. Thank you for believing in me and loving me with every fiber of your enormous heart. I know we will meet again in glory.

And most of all, thank You to Jesus. You walked into the jaws of death, took the keys, and walked out again so that Al and I and all the rest of those who trust in You can live forever. You have walked with me through my dark valley of grief. My worship and love for all eternity will never be enough thanks.

NOTES

Introduction

1. 1 Corinthians 15:54–55, KJV.

Chapter 8—Why, God?

1. Blue Letter Bible, s.v. *"yakach,"* accessed January 2, 2019, https://www.blueletterbible.org/lang/Lexicon/Lexicon. cfm?strongs=H3198&t=KJV.

Chapter 9—Complications of Grief

1. "Suicide Rising Across the US," Centers for Disease Control and Prevention, June 7, 2018, https://www.cdc.gov/ vitalsigns/suicide/index.html.

Chapter 12—Debunking Myths About Death

1. See Albert Einstein, *Relativity: The Special and the General Theory* (New York: Three Rivers Press, 1961).

Chapter 13—Moving Forward Without Your Loved One

1. C. S. Lewis, *The Four Loves* (New York: HarperOne, 2017), 155–156.

DR. CAROL WOULD LOVE TO HEAR FROM YOU!

You can write to her at *drcarolministries.com*.
Join Dr. Carol on her website/blog for many more resources:
www.drcarolministries.com

ABOUT DR. CAROL

Carol Peters-Tanksley, MD, DMin, sometimes known to her friends as "Doctor-Doctor," is a licensed physician and also a Doctor of Ministry. She has practiced medicine for over twenty-five years and is board certified in obstetrics-gynecology and reproductive endocrinology. She currently practices part time so as to devote more time to writing and other ministry efforts.

While continuing to practice medicine, she sought ministry training and completed a Doctor of Ministry degree from Oral Roberts University. She subsequently founded Totally Free Ministries (now Dr. Carol Ministries) as a nonprofit Christian ministry dedicated to helping people discover the Fully Alive kind of life that Jesus came to give each one of us.

Dr. Carol and her husband, Al Tanksley, cohosted the Dr. Carol Show radio program for over five years until shortly before his death in 2016. Dr. Carol also enjoys speaking to church groups, women's groups, and doctors in training, among others.

Dr. Carol makes her home in Austin, Texas, where she enjoys being Grandma Carol to four wonderful grandchildren.

ALSO BY DR. CAROL

Dr. Carol's Guide to Women's Health: Take Charge of Your Physical and Emotional Well-Being brings together medical science, the author's practical experience, and a faith perspective to the full spectrum of physical and mental health issues women face throughout the various seasons of their lives. A healthy woman is so much more than her reproductive organs!

Overcoming Fear and Anxiety Through Spiritual Warfare will help you discover the source of your fear and anxiety and break their hold. You will learn the tools you need to experience improved psychological well-being and engage in spiritual warfare practices that will break the enemy's hold on you. **You can experience the freedom God has for you!**

 @DrCarolT   @DrCarolT   @DrCarolT

DON'T GET OVER IT.
GET THROUGH IT.

AS MY WAY OF SAYING THANK YOU...

I'm so happy you read my book. But the journey doesn't end here. I encourage you to explore beyond what is presented in *The Christian's Journey Through Grief*. So, as both a thank you and a means to learn more, I am offering you a few gifts:

E-book: *The Christian's Journey Through Grief*

E-book: *Overcoming Fear and Anxiety Through Spiritual Warfare*

Devotional Series: Daily devotionals sent to your inbox each day for thirty days

To get these **FREE GIFTS**, please go to
WWW.DRCAROLBOOKS.COM/GIFT

Thanks again, and God bless you.

Dr. Carol Peters-Tanksley

CHARISMA
HOUSE